God Bless You
And may you continue
to see God's Love
with all your Heart.
Sincerely,

Renay Poirier

I Once Was Blind

The Miracle of How Renay Poirier Regained His Sight

"*I Once Was Blind* is a story of divine faith and of its power to heal us of every suffering. Through the account of Renay Poirier's life, especially the tragic loss of his sight in a brief moment through an industrial accident, to the wonderful regaining of his sight, we see how faith, expressed in fidelity to prayer, always brings God's blessings. . . .

"I am confident that all who read Renay's account of his life, especially of the miraculous recovery of his sight, will be inspired to an ever deeper faith and trust in God's never failing mercy."

—Most Rev. Raymond L. Burke
Bishop of LaCrosse, Wisconsin

I Once Was Blind

The Miracle of How Renay Poirier Regained His Sight

Renay Poirier with Jane A. G. Kise

SunCreek
B O O K S

Allen, Texas

Acknowledgments

Scripture texts are taken from the *New American Bible with Revised New Testament and Psalms* © 1991, 1986, 1970. Confraternity of Christian Doctrine, Inc. Washington, D.C. Used with permission. All rights reserved. No portion of *The New American Bible* may be reprinted without permission in writing from the copyright holder.

"Making Magic" Adapted from *Did You Get What You Prayed For?* © 2003 by Nancy Jo Sullivan and Jane A.G. Kise. Used by permission of Multnomah Publishers, Inc.

Front cover photo of Renay Poirier and family photo on back © Elizabeth Flores/Milwaukee Journal Sentinel.

Send all inquiries to:
SunCreek Books
An RCL Company
200 East Bethany Drive
Allen, Texas 75002-3804

Telephone: 800-264-0368 / 972-390-6400
Fax: 800-688-8356 / 972-390-6560

Visit us at: **www.thomasmore.com**
Customer Service E-mail: **cservice@rcl-enterprises.com**

Printed in the United States of America

Library of Congress Control Number: 2003105128

5706   ISBN 0-932057-06-4

1 2 3 4 5   07 06 05 04 03

To my dear sweet wife Connie,
who faced challenges too great in number to mention.
Yet your love conquered all and you kept us
together as a family. In the river of tears
you were my raft and my anchor.

And to my darling daughters Alea and Kara,
who with their tiny hands as toddlers
were my guiding stars and a breath of hope
for my future as a father. I will be grateful to you
till the end of time.

I FEEL THE NEED TO THANK so many yet fear I will never
have enough time or be able to express adequately the
difference they made in my life. I now have the courage to
see myself through loving and accepting eyes. I have never
before and will never again write a book that has opened my
eyes as this one has. I humbly offer my thanks to God, who
each day turns our darkness into light.

A special heartfelt gratitude goes to Bishop Raymond
Burke, Father Klimek, Father Corradi, and all you who keep
faith alive and for guiding my spirit. You are true shepherds.
And to all of the Franciscan Sisters, and Sister Monica and
Sister Barbara, for your hugs of support. I needed them! Also
to Steve Ronstrom for your guidance.

Thanks to my family. To Mom, for devoting her life to her children, under God's roof with God's rules. My brother Randy, for taking and carrying the responsibility of being like a father, a brother, and a friend forever. Sister Rhonda and her husband Greg, for your wide shoulders, wisdom, and quite simply the best pies in the world—you kept me going. Sisters Kim and Shanon, for your smiles of warmth and support I received through the sounds of your voices. My stepfather Wayne and brother John, for your calm sense of listening. And Connie's mom, dad, and family, for enriching our lives throughout times of frustration.

Thanks to all the teachers and staff at Wausau, UWEC, and St. Kate's, especially Susan Nelson, Deb Churchill, and Mary Sue Ingman—I loved to hear you laugh. You helped transform this one life to help many. And to all the students at St. Kate's, especially Deb DeJonge and Pat Schmidt—though I never saw your faces, I could feel the love of Christ through your hearts. Your acceptance of my imperfections assures me of our tomorrow.

To lifelong friends, who remain true: Steve and Lisa Eichinger, Steve Trainor and family, Brett and Amy Spiker—we'll love you always.

To the athletes at pro, collegiate, on down to grade-school level, especially the Packers and the Blugolds. You give our family wholesome opportunities to share great family time and enjoy positive role models. And to Nolan Ryan for the baseball; I felt like God's catcher when I received that fastball.

A special thanks to all the people around the world, who in their time of need reach out and help others in their time of need. You breathe fresh life into our souls. May God continue to bless and touch your hearts with love, allowing you to see through the darkness.

Contents

Introduction

I Once Was Blind . . .

BUILDING, IMPROVISING, using my hands, creating the new, repairing the old . . . it's always been a part of me. From the moment I was old enough to hold a screwdriver, Great-grandfather Albert used to swing by our house in his pickup truck. "Renay," he'd call, "I need a helper in my workshop today," and off we'd go.

On those magical afternoons, "Grandpa" would prop me up on his workbench between a few pieces of wood. From my perch, I watched as he carved delicate scrollwork or sanded the top of a cabinet to perfect smoothness for me to run my hand along. He explained what each chisel, awl, and router was for. Often, he let me grab some of the safer tools so I could work on my own "masterpieces."

One day I watched Grandpa Albert bevel the last edge on a special cabinet he'd built for a business in town. "There, all done but the staining and a final rub with steel wool," he told me. "Let me see if I can find some good rags. I'll be right back, young feller."

I watched him disappear out the workshop door, then I crawled over to the cabinet. I knew I could finish the job for him. Hadn't he shown me how to do everything? Screwdriver in hand, I started to engrave a special design on the top. My pride grew as I saw how easily I could make a deep indentation, just like the scrollwork that often adorned Grandpa's pieces.

Grandpa Albert wasn't gone more than a few seconds. When he returned, I looked up from my work and said, "I'm helping."

Calmly, he walked over and ran his hand across the top of the cabinet. Then he patted my head and said, "I usually initial my work, but I see that this time you did it for me. Thanks, little buddy." Then he placed a small piece of wood in front of me along with a hammer and screwdriver. I carved away while he made some adjustments to the cabinet.

Years later, my mother told me that she couldn't believe Grandpa Albert ever let me back in his workshop again. But he did, although I'm quite certain he never left me alone, even for a millisecond.

Where did he get the wisdom to consciously choose to view my actions through my three-year-old eyes instead of his own? Did working with wood give him that phenomenal wellspring of patience or did it come by the grace of God, from weathering the many storms of life that all of us eventually face?

Family stories about Great-grandfather Albert center on woodworking and worship. His reputation as a master craftsman kept him traveling across the country, taking the train from one job to the next, often staying for weeks in a town as he custom-designed new counters for a store or display cases for a library. And in each town, he found a place to worship, a congregation to join with in prayer. Mother taught us one of the prayers he used to say: "Lord, give me enough strength for my heart to pump the blood of Christ, through all I am, in all my days, so I may help those in need to draw closer to you."

In the first years after my accident, I was one of those in need. Scratched and scarred, wondering whether my life could ever become the kind of masterpiece God envisions for each of us, I cried out for patience, for hope, for the ability to still recognize the beauty all around me. At times, I think God wanted to reach down, pat me on the head, and say, "Thanks, young feller, but let me help you now. I know more about making the patterns of your life than you do."

Stubbornly, I kept a tight hold on the tools I had—my pride, my desire to find my own solutions, my fears that my future held nothing. Outwardly, I continued as a husband and father, striving to reconstruct my life. But inside my heart and soul, I lay rocking in a fetal position, desperate to flee from the silence of solitude, curled up in physical and emotional agony. My attempts to venture forth left me stumbling, overhearing whirling whispers that cut deep like a knife.

Understanding, grasping, and finally accepting a sightless future drove me to my knees, where I, a sinner, belonged. Stretching out my arms, I finally allowed my mind and soul to drift toward heaven. I listened, I heard, I saw that I am loved.

Despite Grandpa Albert's early instruction, I never mastered carpentry. However, I've discovered that when I lay my simple words and my will in the hands of the greatest Carpenter of all, he can work through me to build the City of God on earth. This book isn't about me and how I overcame a disability. Rather, it's about how for years I let the things I couldn't do be my master, until I finally admitted that God is the only master I need. As you read these pages I hope that my God, who reached down and held me until I discovered a new future all carved out for me, comes alive for you.

1

Jesus told us, "In the world you WILL [emphasis added] have trouble." It's guaranteed. "But," he added, "take courage, I have conquered the world."

(John 16:33)

In the Blink of an Eye

SLEEPING BABIES bring serenity to a home. So do secret birthday surprises. The morning of October 9, 1990, silence and secrets made our little home feel like a castle. I remember savoring every moment that morning, the sights and sounds of our life together, as if something inside were calling me to embrace the true treasure that was my family.

Standing in our kitchen, I gazed out the window to where the first rays of sunlight glistened across the rich yellows and oranges of the autumn leaves. For a few weeks each fall, nature made the maples and oaks of northern Wisconsin the fairest sight on earth. No palace garden could be more beautiful.

As I shook the frozen orange juice concentrate into a plastic pitcher, I whispered to myself, "You're no king, but this is like the end of a fairy tale—every dream come true." I'd felt that way all fall, ever since our second daughter was born.

I couldn't help chuckling at the thought of living happily ever after. I'd certainly found my queen, Connie. Tomorrow,

October 10, would be her thirtieth birthday. I'd been planning the celebration for months. Connie wouldn't be getting any singing telegrams or black candles or withered roses. I wanted to celebrate us and all that we had together.

At the top of my list were our two little princesses, asleep in their rooms just down the hall from the kitchen. As I stirred the orange juice, I caught sight of the piles of leaves in our little backyard. The day before, Alea, almost two and a half, must have jumped into those leaves with me three dozen times.

Then there was Kara, barely two months old but already full of smiles. Being a father delighted me, perhaps because I'd never really known my own father. Mom had raised the five of us herself after my dad deserted her, so I was going to be the best dad I could be to my girls.

Thinking of our little house as my castle made me smile. I'd lived in rental housing my whole childhood; now, the 1960s ranch-style house we'd bought the year before seemed like a palace. I'd finished most of the major repairs and Connie kept adding touches to make it "ours." In a few weeks, we planned to lay new carpet, just in time for Kara's baptism party.

Fairy-tale kings and queens didn't have to work as hard as we did, but I loved my position as a senior maintenance technician at Cray Research in Chippewa Falls, Wisconsin. It was one more step up the ladder of the electrician's trade. I'd finished my journeyman apprenticeship. Eventually, I'd be able to start my own business as a master electrician, but I planned to also keep my post at Cray so Connie could stay home with our girls.

Connie had resigned from her teaching position at a local Catholic school in June the year before. As much as Connie delighted in teaching, she loved being a mother. I'd always been haunted by how hard my own mother, a nurse, had worked while trying to raise us, and I hoped to make Connie's life easier.

Connie tiptoed into the kitchen and gave me a good-morning peck on the cheek. I looked at the clock on the old countertop microwave, did a quick calculation, and said, "Your birthday begins in just seventeen hours. Are we going to stay up till midnight to celebrate right from the start?"

Connie reached for the pitcher of orange juice as she replied, "Let's leave that up to Kara. She may have us celebrating at both midnight and dawn."

I don't think either Connie or I had slept through the night since Kara was born. I did the diaper changes and Connie took care of feedings. "You're right, midnight isn't a good idea this year. Let me cook dinner tonight *and* tomorrow to make up for it."

Connie smiled. "And breakfast in bed?"

"With a rose on your tray." I smiled back, thinking of the special present Alea would wrap inside her napkin. The black jeweler's box hidden in my sock drawer held a necklace with two hearts intertwined, a diamond nestled in the middle symbolizing the sparkle of our two daughters in our lives.

Just like every morning, Connie and I ate breakfast together as we talked about our plans for the day. I kept listening for sounds from Alea's room. Often she awoke before I left for work and we had time to read a short book together.

But today she slept on, so I headed for the shower. The bathroom was bare of linoleum; I'd pulled up the old yellowed floor a few weeks earlier. The plastic tiles around the tub needed replacing and the places where I'd already torn out soggy Sheetrock exposed rusty pipes. A buddy would take care of the plumbing work for me in exchange for my electrical expertise sometime in the future.

My renovation plans were hopelessly behind schedule, though. For the last few months, reading stories and preparing backyard picnics and building forts out of pillows and blankets with Alea had won over replacing warped linoleum and ancient pipes. I planned to enjoy the remaining nice days of fall. The home improvements could wait for a below-zero weekend, part of winter in Eau Claire.

Before heading out the door, I always peeked in on the girls. Alea, snuggled up in her favorite ruffled nightgown, looked so tiny in her new big-girl bed. She stirred, opened one eye, and murmured, "I'll see you later. Love you."

"I love you, too. See you later, sweetheart."

We'd built the bed out of solid oak the summer before, crafting a little ladder at the footboard so she could easily climb in and out.

Slowly, I opened Kara's door and smiled as I looked at the wallpaper we'd just finished hanging, with its little blue elephants holding heart-shaped balloons. The hearts on her gown matched the room. I walked over to Kara's crib to make sure she was breathing and, with a gentle pat on her back, said a quick prayer for the day. I was thankful. I really thought I knew how lucky I was.

I met Connie by the front door, we hugged and kissed, and I watched love sparkle in her eye as I said good-bye.

The autumn air had a crisp fall snap to it as I walked out to the maroon '74 Catalina that I'd restored myself. That car almost drove itself for my twenty-minute commute, past stands of crimson maples and golden birch. It would be a great day to work outside.

Being an electrician at Cray was no small task. The multi-building complex used enough electricity to power an entire housing subdivision. Each supercomputer built and tested there weighed 5,000 pounds and used 160 kilowatts of electricity, enough for 160 households. The power came from two dams on the Chippewa River. Behind the systems building was a maze of green steel high-voltage cabinets, transformers, and cables—an electrician's paradise.

Cray had about 3,000 employees and a parking lot sized to hold all of their cars. My shift started early, so I usually found a place just a hundred yards or so from the maintenance building. With the chill in the air that morning, mist from the engineering plant's two huge cooling towers spread along the ground like fog. Walking through the swirling mist was like walking on clouds, I was tempted to peer about for angels.

The maintenance technicians always gathered for a few minutes in the morning for coffee and to discuss our tasks for the day. I walked into the break room and greeted everyone as I stowed my lunch in the fridge, then grabbed a chair by Steve Eichinger, my fishing buddy, better known as Ike.

Some of the men were finishing off microwave oatmeal or muffins as they chatted. Once a month or so, we made breakfast together, each of us contributing eggs or bacon or rolls.

Ike and I drew an inside job that day, running motor generator cables to the 2500-amp main switchboard. The heavy, rubber-coated cables were about three and a half inches in diameter, filled with electrical wires. We wore headsets to guard against the constant noise from the generators, so conversation didn't go beyond shouts of "Grab this" or "More slack," but mornings with Ike always passed quickly.

Around 9:00, everything went silent and dark. We stopped what we were doing and looked around. Had the hydro plants failed or was it a switch gear problem? Either way, I knew we'd be hustling until the problem was solved. Ike and I checked all the equipment in the room where we'd been working, then the other main switch gears we passed as we headed back to the maintenance office to report in.

We were some of the last to arrive. Our boss told us, "Everything's down. I've called the power company and they'll be here any second. Let's watch what they do—we might learn something new about the power cabinets."

"While we're waiting, shouldn't we make sure everything's shut down?" someone asked.

"Of course," he answered, as if that were a given.

Steve and I grabbed a few extra tools from the equipment room and proceeded to close valves on the compressors until the power company arrived. When everything was set, meaning we could run through the proper sequences when the power came back on, we headed outside to the equipment field where power company workers were testing different circuits.

Around noon the senior lineman said, "It's lunchtime, but we know the problem's in switch gear A." I peered past him to where the heavy green door on A's cabinet hung open. As we headed toward his truck, he paused in front of the cabinet and added, "To hook it up, just take this group of wires and put it over there. The power's all off."

My boss said, "Okay."

Looking into the cabinet, the task seemed easy enough. The six thick, insulated wires were already unbolted from one terminal block. I grabbed the bulky bundle of wires with both hands, pulled them toward me a bit to get some slack, then pressed them back to the other terminal. I felt a tingling electrical surge in the air.

In a moment that seemed to last an hour, I saw the spark, the white-hot flash. Then everything disappeared in a thunderous fireball. My head struck against something hard and my world went black.

I knew someone was calling, "Renay, are you all right?" Everything was blurry. I tried to sit up, but pain shot through my back and neck. The blast had thrown me back fifteen feet, into a concrete wall.

Someone grabbed my hand. "Renay?" It was Ike's voice but the shadow of his face seemed distant, as if at the end of a smoke-filled tunnel. With his help, I gingerly moved my arms and legs. Nothing seemed broken, although each limb felt like one big bruise. Ike helped me to my feet and half-carried me back to the maintenance shop. I couldn't see where we were going. The whole world seemed a blur of black and white.

I stumbled as Ike tried to hold open the door for me. "We need help here," he yelled, and I heard voices saying, "Oh, no." "Call 911." "What happened?"

My coworkers gathered around and helped me sit down. One put his hand on my shoulder. "I bet it's welder's eye. You'll be fine in no time." *Lord, let that be true,* I prayed as pain darted through my spine. My head throbbed as if a vice were tightening around it.

Steve drove me to a nearby medical facility. There, a doctor prodded and poked me to make sure I didn't have any broken ribs or internal injuries. X-rays of my back and neck showed some bulging discs. Something had torn in my left shoulder as well, but the doctor said, "You are one lucky guy to walk away from an explosion like that with nothing but bumps and bruises. You're going to be sore for a few days, but compared to what could have happened. . . ."

I dug down to find my voice. "What about my eyes?"

"Your eyes?"

"I can't focus."

"Let me take another look." The doctor pulled out his ophthalmoscope. At least I could sense its penetrating light. After a long time he said, "There are some scratches and burns on the cornea, but don't worry. Your eyesight will return to normal faster than those bruises will fade. But let's bandage them for now to avoid any further irritation."

A pad over each eye, then loop after loop of gauze around my head. Having my eyes covered was actually more comforting than the constant blur.

Steve Trainor, who only lived a mile from me, drove me home. At that moment, I didn't have to see my home to appreciate it. I could picture Alea's pile of leaves, the stack of odds and ends I'd hauled out of the garage the Saturday before, the front room I'd painted only a week ago.

Steve helped me out of the car and up the front steps, opening the screen door while holding my arm. I said, "If you get me to the couch I'll be fine."

Then Connie stepped in from the kitchen where she'd been fixing dinner. "Renay! What happened?" Together, Steve and Connie propelled me to the couch and eased my feet onto a stool as Steve quickly told her about the explosion.

As I listened to him, I wondered how close I'd been to never coming home again. If I'd held the wires a split second longer or hit the concrete at a different angle or . . . but I was home again, thank God.

The thankfulness I'd felt that morning was nothing compared to my overwhelming sense of gratitude that evening as I sat between Connie and Alea, with Kara snuggled against my chest. I'd known that life was precious, but from now on I vowed to appreciate every moment. *God, I know you're in charge. Thanks for saving my life today . . . I give it back to you.*

*God doesn't require that we have the strength
to leap tall buildings in a single bound,
but rather the strength to say,
"I will follow you, Lord."*

2

Entrapped in darkness as I was, instead of visual images of the first week after the accident, my memories wrap themselves around the people who reached out to me.

Darkness Falls

"SOME WAY TO START your birthday, huh? I'll serve that breakfast in bed as soon as I can see to fry an egg," I promised as Connie helped me to the couch the next morning. She squeezed my hand, about the only thing that didn't ache from being hit with 12,500 volts of electricity.

"Your being alive is a present that'll last a bit longer than breakfast in bed," Connie said as she gave me a kiss on the cheek. "Besides, your mom called. She's stopping by with my birthday cake and dinner. I bet I won't have to cook for a week."

I could barely turn my head, let alone give Connie the hug she deserved.

My mother, the nurse, asked a thousand questions. She sat down next to me and rubbed my hand nervously, practically wearing out a spot in my skin. Finally, she asked, "When will you seen an eye specialist?"

I sensed fear in her voice, so I tried to calm her down. "Mom, it's not that bad. In a few days. . . ."

"Don't wait," she replied. "You can't fool with eye injuries."

Baby Kara seemed to cry more, perhaps picking up on the tension in the adults around her. During Kara's colicky moments, Connie laid her across my chest, her favorite sleeping position. I almost welcomed Kara's fussing since I didn't need to see her to enjoy the way she grabbed my finger in her tiny fist, content to hold it as she drifted off to sleep. Besides, it was one of the few ways I could help Connie. Kara didn't quiet down as quickly, though, as she had before the accident. Perhaps I held her more stiffly, unable to move easily with the pain in my neck and back.

Alea thought it great fun to be my helper. "Take my hand, Daddy. I can help you to the table." "Here are your shoes, Daddy. What else?"

Her little mind didn't quite have my troubles all worked out. "Look what I have, Daddy. . . . Oh, your eyes hurt."

"Yes, but they'll be better soon. Let me guess what you're holding. A doll?"

"No, the book about the caterpillar."

"Well, why don't you read it to me?" I rubbed her back as she described the pictures. Punkin, our pudgy, orange tabby cat, often nosed his way in with us, too.

On the phone with her grandparents, Alea proudly announced, "I'm helping Daddy today." And she really was. She even reminded me about the necklace we'd gotten for Connie, late though we were in finally giving it to her.

Ike brought a meal over and stayed to chat. We headed outside to the back porch, my hand on his shoulder to guide me. He asked, "What else can I do?"

"Let's just talk," I said. Already, I felt isolated from my friends. "What's happening at work? Are you going to wait for me to help rewire your cabin?"

We talked about the accident, too. Ike told me that when he saw the flash of fire, he assumed I was dead. "I know you're grateful to be alive," he said, "but . . . if you'd seen it. . . ."

My manager at Cray checked in by phone. "Sure glad it wasn't worse . . . don't feel you have to rush back to work. Take care of yourself."

But I'd never sat still so much in my life. Heading to physical therapy a couple days after the accident was a treat. Connie picked out my clothes and inspected my efforts with the electric razor. "I hope they let me go back to work next week," I said. "I miss it so much and there's so much to do."

"Well, I'm very content to have you just be—here with us," Connie replied. "All four of us safe and alive in our own home."

Almost daily at first, Joan, my therapist, pushed and prodded me, helping me move my neck, arms, and back, working toward a pain-free range of motion.

Not quite a week after the accident, Connie drove me back to the clinic so the doctor could unbandage my eyes. Fifteen minutes in the waiting area, another fifteen sitting in a little room, all the while thinking I could have snipped through the bandages at home and saved all the hassle.

The doctor finally arrived, saying, "I'm going to dim the lights in here. Otherwise, at first you'll feel like you stared right into the sun."

I could feel his scissors slice through the layers of gauze at the back of my head and the cool air against my skin as the bulky patches fell away. I blinked a few times, then reached up to rub my eyes.

"Don't touch them," the doctor cautioned. "Let me check how well the surface scratches are healing. Look straight ahead."

I heard a click as his instrument lit up, but I could barely detect its bright beam. "Everything's still blurry," I said.

"Oh, it'll take awhile to be a hundred percent normal again. Think of how gradually a scratch or burn on your skin heals. That's what we're dealing with here. Now, let's take a look at the eye chart on the back of the door and you can be on your way."

"I can't tell where the door is, let alone the chart," I said, trying to keep the growing concern out of my voice.

Connie asked, "Are there eye drops or. . . ."

"I'll give you a couple of prescriptions, but it looks like the eyes just need another week or so to heal," he said. "Just to make sure I haven't missed anything, here's a referral to an eye specialist."

As I left the clinic, I entered a blurry new world of light and shadows. Without the bandages I felt even less certain of where to put my feet since my brain told me that I *should* be able to see. We drove home in silence.

At first I kept repeating to myself the doctor's cheery prognosis that within the week I'd be able to see again. He'd said there was nothing seriously wrong, yet as the days went by, I began to wonder what he'd missed. Every morning I peered into the bathroom mirror, saying to myself, *Surely you can see your eyebrows, nose, mouth—something!* Then I'd stare at my hand, trying to see my wiggling fingers. Nothing.

The shadow of my own face in the mirror wasn't as hard to bear as the shadowy faces of those around me. It seemed as if they were getting more blurry, not less. It was so hard not to be able to see my girls smile, or catch Connie's special gaze. One morning, as Kara cooed in her crib, I leaned on the railing and stared, willing myself to see her face.

I heard Connie come in. She must have guessed what I was thinking. She gently rubbed the palm of her hand between my shoulder blades and said, "Just a couple more days till we see the eye specialist. Then we'll know what's going on."

My first visit to the ophthalmologist, Dr. Redman, lasted several hours as he ran tests for everything from abnormal pressure in my eyes to retinal damage. Finally, he said, "The physical problems I can detect are the cuts and dry patches on both corneas. They could be sufficient cause for your vision problems. The only cure is time."

Time was one thing I had plenty of. I spent hours sitting on the couch, afraid to walk around for fear that Kara might have rolled around and into my path. I heard Connie scrambling between dinner and diaper changes, unable to help much. I had to tell Alea, "Daddy can't take you outside because I can't see where you are. Here, let's sit on the floor and roll the ball to each other."

The long days were punctuated by another visit to the eye doctor and then another. I seldom left the house, other than for doctor's visits and church. Otherwise, I was too self-conscious about my shuffling gait as I held onto Connie's hand.

Inside, I determined to get around more on my own. With one hand brushing against the hallway wall, I counted out the steps to the kitchen. Three paces from the doorway to the kitchen table. Whoops, a bit to the left or I'd bump into the counter. Turn carefully, four steps, and I was into the living room. Now, across the floor and—I tripped over something. *Oh God, not one of the girls.* I panicked as I fell. But it was Alea's teddy bear. I took a deep breath.

"Okay, Alea," I said, still sitting on the floor. "We need a way for Daddy to stay safe, so can we put these things away?" I tried to make a game out of it, knowing I'd soon be able to see again. I kept reminding myself of that fact.

Then one day I stepped on something soft: a screech of pain, then something ran over my foot. Punkin. I couldn't even see our orange tabby. From then on, Punkin meowed loudly anytime I came near, as if to say, "Please don't hurt me again."

I couldn't deny it any longer. My vision was growing worse, not better. The colors were gone. My world was black and white. When I peered at Alea's face, it was like staring through milky glass. I tried to shield the girls from my despair, but inside I was crying. Connie and I saved our conversations about my eyes for evenings, after the girls were asleep.

Then, long after Connie's breathing slowed into the steady rhythm of sleep, I talked to God. *Are you there? I don't understand . . . are you trying to teach me something, or have I lost touch with where you are, with what you are to me? Please, I need to see . . . don't leave me in darkness. . . .*

Children trust in their parents to safely transport them to and fro. As adults, we question God about roads, maps, gasoline, and directions for our journeys when we should simply seek to trust.

3

In the days following the accident, my heart joined with the psalmist, saying, "I rejoiced when they said to me, / 'Let us go to the house of the LORD.'"

(Psalm 122:1)

Gathering in His Name

THUNK! The heavy Sunday paper had arrived on the front step. Connie opened the front door quietly, trying not to disturb our sleeping daughters. I said, "The Packers game preview section is all yours this morning, honey." My wife knew more about football than I did, even though I'd played quarterback for Bloomer High School.

She joined me on the couch. "This way we can share. I'll read it to you," she said. "We should have at least twenty minutes before the girls wake up. And, since we aren't going to church, we can finish later."

Church. My mind filled with visions of the banner-adorned sanctuary of St. Olaf's. Surrounded by friends, music, and the familiar words of the priest, that hour on Sunday morning always felt like going home to a place of peace.

"Going to church would be a lot of work for you," I said as I shifted the pillow behind my head. I tried to imagine sitting on a hard, wooden pew with my aching neck and bruised back.

"No more than taking the girls to the store. Do you want to go to church?"

I thought for a moment. Did I want people to stare at me while I held onto Connie's shoulder? *Renay, you won't see if they do*, I told myself. Besides, most people already knew of the accident, through the prayer chain.

I said, "I suppose that skipping a week would be okay. Next Sunday I'll probably be able to see again. But . . . we have so much to be thankful for. I think I'd like to go."

"Then I'll start getting ready. As soon as we finish the sports page."

A spark of contentment eased my thoughts. In truth, I was scared of what the next few weeks would bring. In the days since the accident, I'd barely slept—first because of the pain and then because my mind wouldn't slow down. Without any distractions from the sights around me, fearful thoughts swarmed through my brain. How fast would my eyes heal? How long would I be out of work? What would I do with myself until I returned to Cray? None of this fit with my self-image as the strong family man.

I wanted to feel surrounded by God. I couldn't wait to get to church.

Connie picked out my clothes for me, then dressed the girls while I struggled into my pants and shirt. Before we left, Connie gave me a once-over, straightening my collar and brushing a few stray hairs into place. "I don't know how I'll take communion," I said.

"I'll be beside you," she said as she gave my hand a squeeze. "We'll take my car. I feel like a tank commander in your Catalina."

Connie had to make two trips to the car, one with Alea and one with Kara, while I eased myself into the passenger side of the front seat.

As we made the seven-minute drive to St. Olaf's, I prayed, *Lord, I'm taking this darkness as a chance to grow closer to you. Help me to feel your peace, that you are with me.*

Our sanctuary was built as a gym for the attached school—the parish couldn't afford both. But the painted cinder-block walls are marked with crosses made by brick indentations. Colorful banners often adorn the walls, changing with the seasons. The wooden pews complete the impression of a place of worship; for now, gym classes take place in the school cafeteria or outside.

When we arrived, Connie gently helped me to my feet, then unbuckled Alea's car seat. "Hold Daddy's hand while I get Kara," she said.

Alea's little hand grasped mine. I placed my other hand on Connie's shoulder as soon as Kara was in her arms. I imagine we made quite a procession, but all I noticed was Alea. As we walked through the parking lot toward the wide double doors at the back of the sanctuary, she guided me like a shepherd. "Be careful, Daddy. This way, Daddy." She was only two and a half, caring for me when I should have been caring for her.

Connie led me to our usual pew, about four from the back on the left. I lowered myself gingerly onto the hard wooden seat, then whispered to Connie, "Can I take Kara now?"

As our baby snuggled in against me, I could feel her little heart fluttering. Kara was still so tiny, yet in holding her, I felt love. The love of our family, God's love, Christian fellowship, all surged around me.

I settled back into the pew, determined to enjoy what my other senses could tell me about the service. During the hymn I listened to all the different voices surrounding me. There were so many sounds: the echoing of the benches before and after we knelt to pray, books being shuffled into position at the ends of the pews, the whistling of the wind when someone opened the outside door during mass. The last sound seemed like the presence of the Holy Spirit as I sat in my unaccustomed darkness.

At one point, while the choir was singing, I heard the voice of a little child next to me. "Mommy, where's Jesus?" I didn't hear a reply.

A little later, the same child poked me in the leg. "Hey, Mister. Can you give me my crayon? I dropped it."

I moved my foot across the floor to see if I could feel the crayon and answered, "I'm sorry, I can't find it. But . . . I know where Jesus is."

"Really?"

"Sure, he's in your heart."

I heard him whisper my answer back to his mother. I don't know if he ever found his crayon, but later his mother thanked me for my words. There was still light in the midst of my darkness.

For communion, Alea gently led me out of the pew. Holding Kara with one hand, I again placed my other hand on Connie's shoulder. Connie received the bread first, then waited until Father Menzel placed mine in my hand before turning to leave. I filled my mind with images of other couples holding hands, the young and the old worshiping together, toddlers in their parents' arms gazing at the candles and banners in wonder. I said a silent prayer of thanks that we were still a family.

After the service, our friends crowded around us, asking how I was doing. I couldn't tell if they were talking to Connie or to me. My head started to hurt as I tried to guess how they were directing their questions. I didn't want to be rude by talking out of turn. I fiercely wanted to blend in normally, yet longed to step aside rather than make a mistake that would draw attention to myself.

Then a huge, strong hand grasped my shoulder. Father Menzel. "Renay, I'll pray for you. Are there special prayers I can say?"

Suddenly, the love and concern of our community at St. Olaf's calmed me to the very core of my soul. I wasn't at all alone in the dark. "Just that all of us let Jesus be our guide. Connie, the girls, me . . . that we give him our fears."

Church was just about the only place I ventured in those first weeks, other than doctor and physical therapy appointments. At first, going anywhere didn't seem worth the bother of stumbling over unfamiliar terrain. Soon, I thought, I'd have my sight back and would be able to catch up on errands and friendships. But as the weeks went by and my eyesight showed no signs of returning, I grew even more uneasy about venturing out. It was so much work for Connie, helping me and holding onto the girls. Every trip made me keenly aware of my inadequacies.

Going to St. Olaf's that first Sunday made it easier to keep going. And I needed that hour every week, especially as the darkness continued and my fears mounted. I prayed, *Jesus, I don't know when or if things will get better. Hold me in your comfort and guide me through my fears. Be my light. . . .*

NOVEMBER 3 was approaching, my sister Shanon's birthday, the day of Kara's baptism, scheduled long before my accident. The entire family was invited back to our house after the 5:15 Saturday mass.

We never did get the new carpet installed for the party, but that Saturday morning we awakened to an inch of snow on the ground. Connie said, "It looks like the angels put down a pure white carpet for Kara's day."

Connie laid out blue pants and a pastel plaid shirt for me, then slipped into her long red dress. Alea danced about us in her pink party frock, full of questions as Connie readied

Kara in the same long, lacy white gown that Connie, then Alea, had worn for their baptisms. Alea asked, "Did I look like that, Mom? Was I happy or did I cry when I was baptized?"

"Alea, you were an angel," Connie replied. I heard her kiss Alea's cheek.

We arrived about forty-five minutes before the service so I could practice where to walk and stand. This time we sat in the first pew, right in front of the baptismal font. I practiced so many times that I still remember: five paces to the front step, up two steps, and I was right by the font. I just had to remember where the flower arrangements were.

The practice time gave Alea a chance to check things out. She stared at the octagonal wooden font. "It's like a tiny pond," she said. "Kara will want to swim in it."

Then the service began. The pianist played a song that was new to me and I listened to the words as the soloist sang the first verse:

I heard the voice of Jesus say, I am this dark world's light.
Look unto me, your morn shall rise,
And all your day be bright.
I looked to Jesus and I found in him my star, my sun
And in that light of life I'll walk
till traveling days are done.
(Horatio Bonar 1808-1889. Michael Joncas. GIA Publishing, © 1998.)

In the darkness of the past few weeks, had I really looked to God for light? I'd prayed for God to heal my eyes, all the time singing praises for simply being alive, but had I *listened* for God since the accident? *Lord, be my sun*, I prayed.

As we walked forward for the baptism, I caught just a flash of the bright green of Father Menzel's robes. Father Menzel is over 6' 5", yet he has a gentle, whispering voice.

I handed Kara to him, sensing how his huge hands completely surrounded her. To me, it seemed as if I were placing my child directly into the caring hands of God.

As we spoke the words of faith like millions of parents before us, my heart latched onto Father Menzel's words, ". . . accept God into your lives completely and keep that light burning at all times. God will be your beacon forever."

His words bounced back and forth in my mind. After almost four weeks of darkness, a month without seeing the face of this child we were placing in God's keeping, I wondered where God's light was leading me.

Through the rest of the service, I held Kara close, picturing in my mind's eye a very tiny, beautiful girl in a cloud of white, a gown that held her tight within our faith. Ignoring the tears that slid past one another down my cheeks, I heard the music of her gentle coo in a sort of symphony with our friends and family who cared so deeply about her. I caught the aroma of candles burning on the altar, symbols of the light of Christ that would lead her. Every word of the service seemed directed at me. "Shepherd me, O God, beyond my wants, beyond my fears. . . ." "The light of God surrounds us, the love of God enfolds us. . . ." I prayed, *Lord, please be my light. . . .*

After the service, everyone swarmed around us. "Your girls look so beautiful." "Alea is certainly a wonderful big sister." "God go with you."

Then I felt Father Menzel's strong hand grasp mine. He gave it a firm squeeze and said, "Renay, everything will be okay."

At his words, something deep within me relaxed. It was as if I'd been hanging out a window, grasping the ledge in desperation, only to have God take me by the hand and say, "It's all right. I've got you." My fears diminished in the sensation of relaxing in the hands of God. At that moment

I admitted how frightened I was for our future and how much I needed God. *Okay, God,* I said as we made our way out of the sanctuary, *I'll let my faith see for me.*

Back home, our little house seemed to swell with the family presence of joy, hope, peace, and love. I stayed seated most of the time, listening to the voices and laughter of celebration. We were all together, still.

Alea exercised her right as big sister to help open presents and I listened to her squeals as she and Punkin romped through the ribbons and paper. Kara tried some of her cake, or at least smeared a fistful over her face, from what I could tell as I kissed her.

Mom sat close to her newest granddaughter and exclaimed, "Beautiful girls in pretty dresses, a family with God, and cake to boot—it doesn't get any better than this!"

That night, as we calmed our toddler and rocked our baby, the celebration of being together out-shone any concerns about the future. Sighted or not, the best part of any one of us is the spirit of God within us, and that I still had, burning bright.

Who am I if I have not blessed another or felt the blessings of others through the journey we call Life?

4

During the next weeks, the image I'd received sustained me: I wasn't about to plummet to the ground. I was in God's grasp, not alone in the grip of darkness.

Fading Hopes, Fading Dreams

DOCTOR REDMAN sent me to another specialist in Minneapolis. He repeated several tests, then gave me a dye injection so he could track the blood flow in and out of my eyes. I could hear him shuffling papers as he told Connie and me, "The extensive tests didn't reveal any abnormalities other than the surface scars noted by Dr. Redman. I'm sorry, but there aren't any treatments or procedures I can recommend."

At my next appointment with Dr. Redman, he checked the surface of my eyes again, ran another test, then said, "I'm waving my hand about a foot from your face. Can you see it?"

"There's a . . . a blur."

I heard him sigh as he sat down in his chair. "Renay, I can't pinpoint the problem, so I can't prescribe any treatment."

"So what can we do?" I asked.

"Well, I can't see waiting any longer to get you into a rehabilitation program for the visually impaired. You can't imagine all the ways they can. . . ."

"If you say there's nothing wrong, my sight has to come back," I said.

"I didn't say there wasn't anything wrong. The eye is so delicate, and so complex in how it communicates with the brain, that sometimes we just can't detect what is wrong."

But I was barely listening. Dr. Redman had just voiced what I already knew. I was blind. If I was Renay with the white cane, where was Renay the electrician? Renay the father? The provider? The husband? The friend? Darkness closed in even tighter around me, as a snake squeezes its prey. I felt my future fading away.

Lord, are you still holding onto me? I wondered. Let me feel your grasp once again. From the depths of my despair I call to you . . . please listen, help me trust in your word and know that your love is constant.

CONNIE HEARD every word of Dr. Redman's final prognosis. She waited a few days before she brought up an obvious decision we faced. One of us needed to work. "I'll just get my name on the list for substitutes in a couple of towns close to home. That will help with bills, I don't have to work any day that the girls need me, and you can concentrate on your physical therapy needs until you can go back to work."

Reluctantly, I agreed. What choice did I have? Although my manager at Cray had stated clearly that a job was waiting for me when I had the doctor's okay to return to work, nothing specific had been offered. *I didn't know what I was going to do.*

In those early months, if Connie left the house, I didn't trust myself to watch our girls alone. Connie shuttled them off to a sitter, which left me sitting in an empty house.

Friends called, but they also worked—and I longed to join them. Being home, wondering about my future, was no vacation. Instead, I had empty time on my hands, time to think about all the jobs I'd had and to worry about whether I'd ever find meaningful work again.

I'd worked every day of my life since I was old enough to stay on my bike while tossing newspapers along my route. Actually, my older brother Randy and I started earning money before that. To buy the bike, which we shared, we set our alarm clock for the middle of the night so we could search the yard by flashlight for worms and night crawlers to sell to fishermen early in the morning. The town baker advanced us small cartons to hold our merchandise, letting us pay him back once we'd sold our wares.

It wasn't all work, for if we couldn't quite sell all the worms, well, we had to use them up ourselves! An afternoon at Duncan Creek could yield a hefty dinner of brook trout. Mom counted on us to bring home fish and anything else we could hunt or catch to fry up or boil in the soup kettle. Things were that tight, yet we scarcely knew it because of the love Mom poured into our days.

Once we had the bike, we could finish our paper route in lightning time. Taking aim with folded newspapers, angling for fish, and scooping up earthworms was much more like play than work to Randy and me, especially since Mom needed our help so badly. We insisted that Mom take part of the money, but a bit was ours.

We learned the pleasure of tasting the fruit of our labor— or, in our case, pizza. I'd climb on the handlebars of our Schwinn while Randy pedaled off to the neighborhood pizza place, "Mom's." We'd peel every penny and nickel we had saved out of our pockets and place them in a pile on the counter. I'm sure that the lady who took our order was Mom herself, Mrs. Bleskacek. She smiled as she counted our coins. Drooling in anticipation of the monstrous nine-inch pizza that would soon be ours, we stood speechless in the corner, waiting, while it baked. Then I'd jump back on the handlebars, one hand on the pizza box, one on the bike, while Randy guided us through the roughest, toughest terrain—or so it seemed at the time. We never lost a pizza.

We carried that most precious of cargoes into the refrigerator box from the hardware store that served as our tent. Once inside, off came the box lid and our teeth melted into first bites of cheese and tomato and a paper-thin yet substantial crust. The spicy fragrance permeated the air, lingering until we awoke with the morning sun. At times I swear I can still smell the aroma.

Once a year, we borrowed a burlap bag and nets from Grandpa Meier, my mother's father, and biked out past the edge of town to Duncan Creek for the sucker run. Getting there just after dawn was the best time. Within minutes, our bag would be full of fish. Into the bike basket it'd go and we'd dash home to drop them off before starting our paper route.

One time we had so many fish that they kept falling to the road. One of our customers was out watering the lawn. As I placed the paper on his front porch, right where he liked to find it, he said, "Did you notice all the fish on the street this morning? Isn't it strange?"

Wondering if he'd guessed the truth, I replied, "Very strange. I'll dispose of them if you'd like." He gave me a plastic bag and all was well.

Thus, work and play had always blended in our minds. Often after school, Mom greeted us with rakes and the message, "Mrs. Cronin and Mrs. Kransfelder next door need some help." Off we'd go, glad to be outside and aware that there'd probably be a few cookies waiting when we finished.

Mom told us, "We help others because someday we may need help."

I started working nearly full-time before I finished high school. When Mom remarried, we moved out of Bloomer, but I wanted to finish my senior year in town and play quarterback for my football team. So I roomed with a farmer, Barry Dietsche, on the outskirts of town, doing chores to pay my way.

Barry talked a lot with me about my future. He offered to sell me his second farm, but I was already interested in electrical work. I'd taken an electronics class during my junior year of high school and really enjoyed it. Barry introduced me to an electrician he had hired to do some work around the farm. The electrician asked me if I wanted to work with him on weekends.

The work intrigued me; electricians were always needed. They got to help people solve problems, using their expertise for things their customers couldn't do themselves. I was hooked. College never entered my mind.

But to become an electrician, you have to navigate the trade union. It helps to know someone in order to get an apprenticeship, the first step toward becoming an electrician.

I spent four years on the waiting list while I worked at J. H Larson, an electrical wholesaler/distributor in Eau Claire. The position didn't count toward professional certification, but I gained some experience. Ken Rinholen, the warehouse supervisor, hired me to moonlight with him. We mostly worked jobs on farms, nights and weekends, and I enjoyed the smell and taste of home-cooked feasts from Beatrice, his wife.

Ken expected us to work hard, but he pitched in shoulder-to-shoulder with his crew. One day Ken got us all together. "All of you work as a team. Many's the night I'm simply amazed at how much you accomplish together. I'm proud of you. Teamwork is so important."

Later that day, I watched Ken tumble to the ground from a forklift. He'd had a massive heart attack. The emergency workers let me ride in the ambulance with him, but even as I prayed for God to protect him, I knew Ken was leaving us.

Without Ken, I wondered if my career dreams were over and whether I should pursue something else. Then . . . I think Someone wanted me to be an electrician.

My phone rang—my foreman's brother was very ill. Did I want to take his place on a hunting trip to Colorado? "But I don't own a gun right now."

"You can borrow mine. I'll bring it over." So I borrowed some hunting supplies and a pup tent, piled into a truck with six strangers, and headed for a base camp in the Rocky Mountains.

Being the stranger in the group, I volunteered to take one of the hunting spots farthest from camp. I spent most of the first day trying to reinforce my tent and dry out my gear after a twenty-inch snowfall, but the second day, I made it out to a meadow marked by a deer/elk trail. Around noon, a flash of light caught my eye—the gun or eyeglasses of another hunter, far across the meadow?

A whistle in the wind urged me, *Go and talk to him, make sure you're not in his territory somehow.*

I made my way across the meadow toward the only human within miles, a gentleman sitting on a log. He introduced himself and said, "I'm from Wisconsin. Camping up here with no electricity is a great vacation from my electrical business."

I said, "My dream is to be an electrician, but I've been on the apprenticeship list for four years."

"I think you could probably work for me next year if you still want to," he told me. I gave him my phone number, not really expecting it to lead to anything.

A year later, almost to the day, he called just as he had promised. "Come to work tomorrow. . . ." I gave my two weeks' notice at J. H. Larson and started my apprenticeship.

SITTING AT HOME, alone in the dark, I couldn't quite grasp that the career I'd fought so hard to begin might be over. I'd worked for years to make my way up the ladder, changing electrical jobs only to get closer to home and to my bride-to-be. I was dreaming about getting my master's license, and owning my own business, when the accident happened. With the investment of all those years, the thought of losing my career tore at my heart.

I wanted to work, Connie wanted to be a full-time mother, and instead everything was topsy-turvy. If Connie had the day off, my time was filled with learning to change diapers and poke spoons into baby food jars in my new dark world. More often, I was alone, pouring out my troubles to poor Punkin the cat.

Connie constantly encouraged me, "The girls love the extra time you have with them now." I loved the extra time with them, too, but my friends were all working the eight-to-twelve-hour days I was used to putting in. I felt isolated, cut off from all I knew. I couldn't drive, I couldn't work.

Then one afternoon, Connie and a friend were talking in the kitchen. I overheard the friend say, "I feel for you…it must be like taking care of a third child."

A hot pain, like a knife, slashed through my stomach. Hearing someone say out loud the thoughts I'd been hiding from myself for so long tore through the core of who I wanted to be.

I tried hiding my despair, but one afternoon I sprawled out on our couch and gave in to the tears I'd held back for so long. The next thing I felt was little Alea's hands on my face, her lips kissing my eyes. She said, "Don't worry, Daddy. God's taking care of you."

I hugged her and prayed, *God she's right. I'm alive, I have my family, I have you. But I need help. How can I be useful again?*

Within each of us, the Spirit of God waits, ever ready to supply enough love for our hearts to swell to proportions unimaginable.

5

The Bible tells us that to be happy in our work is a gift of God (Ecclesiastes 5:19). Working as an electrician had been such a gift, but had God taken it back? No, I kept telling myself. Even though I trusted God, I still wondered who I was, now that I wasn't an electrician anymore.

Back to Work

IT WAS JUNE, about eight months after the accident, when my manager from Cray called right in the middle of the day. My heart pounded with joy when he said, "Renay? Hey, how are you? I've found you a job if you're still looking.

"The doctors have to approve this, but we'd love to have you back. There are things you could do. I mean, laying cables in a computer bay would be safe, changing florescent light bulbs, putting in tile, routing wire cables, sorting different size wire connectors and developing an organization strategy for the maintenance department—there must be at least ten things you can do."

Shortly after my accident, he and I had started discussions about work that would benefit Cray as well as be meaningful to me. Finally, he had worked out the details. We discussed transportation issues and worked together to contract with a cab company to get me to and from the plant in Chippewa Falls each day. I couldn't wait to have a reason to gulp down breakfast again and hurry out the door. I assured him that I had the return-to-work approval from my doctor.

"Just think of all the tasks that need more than two hands," he said. "You'll start by accompanying one of the junior maintenance workers and we'll keep adding to your responsibilities."

Connie helped me set my alarm clock the night before my first day back and I listened to her rustle through the closet to find my work clothes. "Exhilarated" wasn't too strong of a word to describe my feelings. The next day I'd be away from the silence of our home during the day, back in the world of people with jobs and responsibilities and futures. I felt my way over to the dresser, checking for my name tag and wallet. Connie said, "Everything's there. We laid it all out."

I turned toward her voice and said, "I know, but I'll never fall asleep unless I check through it again. I feel like the first day of junior high, where you do everything you can to make sure you don't get lost in the halls or trip over your shoelaces."

The next morning, I barely tasted my breakfast in my haste to get to work. I waited for the cab, pacing our little sidewalk, then sitting on the front steps. My heart hammered in my chest as I wondered, *Where is the cab? Did Cray change its mind? Will I be late getting to work? Aren't they picking me up?*

Connie called to me through the window, "Give it time. They aren't as late as you were early getting out there!"

The cab finally pulled into the driveway. It felt strange, climbing into the back seat of a car. I set my lunchbox on the seat beside me and cracked the window just a bit. As the driver pulled onto the highway, I tried to remember each curve in the road. I felt the wind on my face and leaned back, thinking, *Yes this is the first day of the rest of my life. I will do the best I can.*

It turned out that feeling the wind against my face was a good way to start the day. Like every other morning at Cray, I headed first for the break room, grinning just at the sound of men's voices again. Images from the past flooded my mind. But walking into that room for the first time in nine months let me know how much things had changed. Instead of inside jokes or questions about my weekend, the room went silent.

Three of my old buddies greeted me. It felt good to hear their voices. First to my side was Steve Eichinger, saying, "Welcome, welcome back! You're my extra pair of hands today." That was good news. We decided that for starters, I would push the cart while he guided it. Together, we made sure my lunchbox was over toward one side of the fridge shelf so I could find it again.

A few of my old buddies patted me on the back with phrases like, "Good to see you." "Hey, don't overdo it today." Compared to the break room nine months before, though, there were few words.

As the day wore on, I found out that pushing a cart wasn't as easy as it sounded. I ran into empty boxes and wall corners when I could have sworn I turned wide. With each jolt, things fell off. And getting myself around was next to impossible. I'd step to the side to hand a bulb to Steve and trip over a desk chair being stored in a hallway, or an extra stool that someone planned on using.

By the end of two days, I considered wearing shin guards. All I could think was, "How many electricians does it take to change a light bulb?" Who was I kidding? This wasn't a job, but a bone thrown to a dog.

Still, being at work was better than being home alone. Don Olson, a groundskeeper, and Len Cesaffky prayed with me daily. That helped build my spirits even as I realized how little I could do in comparison to before the accident.

At first, I tried orienting myself to all of the hallways. After all, I'd worked in those buildings for years. But I couldn't afford to make mistakes and walk into the wrong rooms; some were "clean rooms" for assembling computer parts. I had to be with someone all the time unless I was just sorting parts.

One afternoon, Steve and I were changing light bulbs in a motor generator room, where the main power flowed into the building. I'd hand him a bulb or an air filter, then he'd hand me the used one and I'd place it in a box on a cart that was just a few steps away.

Suddenly Steve screamed, "Stop!" I froze in my tracks until he grabbed my arm and pulled me toward him.

"Someone left a switch gear open," he said, his voice sounding shaken. "You were about eighteen inches from being toast. If I hadn't finished with that filter and turned around. . . ." Both of us had to sit down for a bit to settle our nerves.

Another time, I was just pushing cables through an opening in the floor. I moved a little to the side—and fell into another hole where more floor tiles had been removed.

Eventually, I spent more of my time in the maintenance shop, organizing supplies. One of the other assistants helped me work out a storage system, and I could feel my way along the bins and find what was needed.

The days went by fast and I relived them throughout the night. I kept telling myself that with all of the little things that I took care of, the electricians had more time to do the real work. Yet . . . was I pulling my weight yet?

I asked Ike that question one afternoon as we ate lunch together. "I'm doing so little compared to before, yet it's all I can do."

"Renay," he said, "you've picked up half a dozen new tasks in the last few weeks, each one more complicated than the last. Give yourself time, you've got to crawl before you walk. We're all cheering for you."

"Thanks," I said as we headed back to the maintenance shop. I hoped he was right. *God, help me, please, if he isn't.*

Sometimes the greatest challenges are the small persistent, daily challenges to our character.

6

*More than anything, I longed to understand
how God could still use me.*

A Breath of Hope

"GOOD MORNING, Renay," my cab driver said.

"Good morning, Tom—you're Tom, right?" I replied as I felt for the passenger door handle. "Did you catch the football game last night?" Tom was the father of one of my high-school classmates. With a population of only 50,000, Eau Claire had just three cab companies. In no time, I knew most of my drivers.

At first, the cab ride arrangements went smoothly—pickups at 7:30 and 4:30 each day—but after a few weeks, my ride after work seemed to come later and later. Finally, after three days of not being picked up until 5:00, I called to make sure there wasn't a schedule mix-up.

The next day, I headed outside at 4:30, thinking that I wouldn't mind the half-hour wait on such a beautiful June day, but the cab drew up along the curb before I could stretch out on the grass. "Thanks," I said as I climbed in. "My girls will be glad to see me on time tonight."

As the driver made the final turn toward my home, he slowed the car, then halted. "There's someone standing in the middle of the road," he explained, "waving for us to stop."

I listened as the driver rolled down his window. "Can you call 911 on your radio?" a man's voice said. "That car in the ditch, there. . . . I think the passenger is having a heart attack."

I leaned forward. "I know CPR. I'm visually impaired, but if you could lead me over there, I think I can help."

Before my hand found the handle, the man opened my door and helped me out of the cab. "It's just a short way down this bank, which isn't very steep," he said. I grabbed a tight hold on his arm and he led me over pavement, then gravel, then grass, for perhaps twenty feet. As we hustled along, he said, "I was following behind them—two women—and the car began swerving, then veered right off into the ditch. I think the driver is the woman's daughter."

He led me to the passenger side of the car and said, "Door's open, right in front of you." I grabbed the door, walked around it, felt for the passenger, all the while trying to recall the details of my CPR training. *How can I do this? Who's going to help me? God help us if I'm her only chance. . . . Who is she? God give me the strength to go on.* I could hear the driver saying, " Someone's here to help now . . . it's going to be all right. . . ." I felt along the back of the seat until I found the woman's shoulder. She was slumped over toward the driver. I asked, "Do you know her very well?"

A young-sounding voice said, "She's my mother."

"How long has she been like this?"

The driver's voice cracked as she answered, "Maybe a minute."

I felt for the release lever on the passenger seat, gently pushed the seat into more of a reclining position, then grabbed hold of the woman's shoulders to pull her to a straighter position. "Hello," I said. "Can you hear me, can you tell me if you're feeling any pain?"

She didn't respond. I felt her neck for a pulse, then her wrist. Was there a heartbeat or just nervous twitches? I couldn't start CPR with a heartbeat. She wasn't breathing. I tilted her head back and leaned over to give her a couple of breaths, then checked her neck again. Still no pulse.

By this time I could hear more voices around the car. "Can someone help me move her to the ground?" I asked.

"Geez, we might get sued. . . ." "No, I can't lift anything. . . ." different bystanders muttered. The truck driver said, "Sorry, back injury."

I called out for the cab driver. "I don't know. . . ." he hesitated, just inches from me. I grabbed for his arm and said, "Yes, *you can help me.* Here, I'll swing her legs around. You lift her there, and I'll get under her shoulders."

The cab driver said, "This man is blind. Can someone help guide him?" The truck driver said, "Sure," and grabbed my shoulder. Together we maneuvered the woman to a flat spot by the side of the road where some of the bystanders had spread out their coats for her.

I crouched down, felt for a pulse once more, then knelt by her side. Soon my thoughts blurred in the rhythm of performing CPR. *Count one, one thousand, two, one thousand . . . push . . . push . . . glide my hand up her arm, lean over to give her two breaths. . . .* I almost felt a part of her, joining with the person in her fight for life, fighting together for it. I was breathing for her, but felt a breath of hope for me . . . pumping her blood, but filling my need to be needed.

As I pushed, I felt an urge to keep talking. "It is such a beautiful day. I'd love to meet your family."

I'd taken my first CPR class back in high school and, as an electrician, I'd had plenty of refresher courses. The last one was at Cray not long before my accident. I'd even been called on to use it one other time, when a woman collapsed at a restaurant. One of the things the instructors emphasize is that performing CPR takes a great deal of physical energy, but that day I felt as if I could go on forever. I remember thinking, *Of all the people here, you're the only one who knows how to do this. Finally, you're doing someone some good.*

Five minutes passed before the wail of sirens filled the air. A police officer knelt beside me. "Keep going while I attach an oxygen mask," she said.

Moments later another siren announced the ambulance's arrival. As the paramedics hurried toward us, the cab driver told them, "He's blind."

I felt a hand on my shoulder. "Do you know her?" one of the paramedics asked me.

I said no and he answered, "You're doing great. Keep it up just a little longer while we set up." Boxes snapped open and paper ripped.

"Okay, we'll take over," the man said. He pulled me away so suddenly that I lost my balance and fell backward. The truck driver helped me to my feet. We stood by while the paramedics worked on her, feeling helpless as the lady fought for her life. One of the paramedics called, "One, two, three . . . clear!" as the jolt of the defibrillator filled the air. I thought in wonder, *How ironic it is that an electrical charge took my life away and here it might restore life in another.*

My heart slowed and I calmed down as I interceded for this person whose life I shared yet didn't know.

A paramedic said, "We've got enough of a pulse to transport her."

"Can I accompany her?" I asked.

"Sorry, even family members need to follow in another vehicle. If you hadn't been around, she wouldn't have had a chance."

As the ambulance drove off, the truck driver said, "Let's get your things. I'll take you home."

Home was just up the hill. The whole incident was over in perhaps fifteen or twenty minutes. The truck driver led me to my own front door and I let myself in, but I couldn't sit down. Too much adrenaline pulsed through me as I thought about everything I knew of heart attacks. I'd started CPR within just a few minutes of when the woman's daughter indicated she'd collapsed. The hospital was just minutes away. *I hope she makes it. How frightened her family must be. How different the events could have gone if my cab had been late, like the previous few days!*

The garage door opened. Connie said, "Did you just get home?"

"Maybe ten minutes ago," I replied.

"Then why are you still carrying around your lunchbox?"

I told her what had happened and said, "I wish I knew whether or not the woman is okay."

"Did you try calling the hospital?" Connie quickly pulled out the phone directory, dialed, then handed me the receiver. The first hospital we tried hadn't had any heart attack admissions in the last half-hour, so we called Sacred Heart Hospital.

"Are you a relative?" the receptionist asked. I told her that I'd given emergency CPR. After a pause she said, "I can't give out names, but we admitted someone."

I let out a whoop. "Yes! She's still alive, Connie, she's alive." My being there had actually mattered.

That night the phone rang. "Renay Poirier?" a woman's voice said. "I believe you're the man who helped my mother today."

"Yes," I said. "How is she?"

"Oh, we are so grateful to you. She's still unconscious, but the doctors have hope for her."

The family called me every day. I finally learned her name, Josie Johnson, and that she was seventy-eight years old. The next morning, Josie woke up but couldn't move. On the third day, the daughter said, "Mother is very weak, but we've all had a chance to talk to her. And we're hoping you'll come down to the hospital so she can say thank you personally."

"I'd love to after work tomorrow, but I'm visually impaired."

"I'll meet you in the lobby. Just come to the main entrance."

Connie drove me to Sacred Heart Hospital. I was out of the car before Connie came around to my side. She walked me through the lobby door, but almost immediately a voice said, "Are you the one?" and a pair of arms enfolded me.

Then another voice said, "Renay? What are you doing here? Remember me, Joan? Your physical therapist?"

I held out a hand in greeting and said, "What are you doing here?"

"The woman you saved was my grandmother!"

Connie stayed in the hospital lobby while Josie's daughter led me to the critical care unit visitors' room. Inside, about ten members of Josie's family were waiting for me. They told me she'd slipped back into a coma. "But," one of her sons said, "every single one of us has had a chance to talk with her. It means so much to me—to all of us—that she didn't die alongside the road."

"She seemed so happy," his sister added. "Mom is always thinking of everyone else. She had something special stored away to say to each one of us, and she got the chance, thanks to you."

I asked if I could see Josie. They checked with her nurse, who then led me into her room where the air was thick with the smell of medicine. Carefully, I felt along the bed railing and located her hand. I could hear nurses talking, machines beeping, water running, and shallow breaths of that someone special, almost a whispering. "Josie," I said softly, "I think everyone in your family has thanked me for helping you. But I want to thank you. You gave me a chance to make a difference to someone again. Thanks. I'll see you again someday."

The rest of the world seemed to disappear as her pulse and mine assumed the same rhythm. My tears welled over, knowing that she was still here because of me.

"Oh my," the nurse exclaimed. "Her heart rate got stronger as you spoke."

I gave Josie's hand a little squeeze as I thanked God for the opportunity not just to see her but to help her and her family. *This is life, God seemed to reply. Things seem to be going so well, then you're knocked down in a moment of time and your dreams of tomorrow are gone. Find new dreams. What happened, happened. Live in the here and now, cherish that moment.*

The whole visit lasted perhaps thirty minutes. I sensed that a part of Josie was already headed toward God, but a part of her would remain with me forever.

Josie's daughter called me when she died. My heart dropped into my stomach, for I'd been so at peace during my time with her, as if God had joined us in those moments. "Can I do anything?"

Her daughter drew a deep breath. "She's in a great place now, shining her light on us."

I told her that heaven had smiled on us when we were together. I wasn't the only one whose life had changed in a second. Now, though, I knew that despite the changes, my life wasn't over. I could still be useful.

I told Connie, "Being an electrician wasn't about wires and circuits, but about lending a hand. People needed my services and I could fix their problems. In helping Josie, I was of service to her and her family."

"You'll find a way, Renay," Connie said. Then she reminded me of one of her favorite Bible passages:

> *Though young men faint and grow weary,*
>> *and youths stagger and fall,*
> *They that hope in the LORD will renew their strength,*
>> *they will soar as with eagles' wings;*
> *They will run and not grow weary,*
>> *walk and not grow faint.*
>
> (Isaiah 40:30–31)

After my conversations with Josie's family I had a renewed hope in the Lord. *God, I trust that you'll show me the path to being useful once again. Amen.*

One cannot live adequately in the present
nor effectively face the future if one's
thoughts are buried in the past.

7

The first place I wanted to be more useful was at home. The gratitude of Josie Johnson's family bolstered my courage, daring me to try to help Connie in any way I could.

Lasagna in the Dark

THE OLD FARMHOUSE washtub loomed large in the basement of my childhood home, and in my memories. While my mother ran the clothes through the wringer, Randy and I took turns standing on a chair and turning the handle, or catching the clothes and placing them in the hamper. Mom carried the heavy basket out to the line, where the two of us helped her shake out the shirts and towels, handing up clothespins as she needed them.

Because my mother was a single working parent, she trained us early on to be her assistant chefs, gardeners, cleaners, and launderers. And once we mastered any household chore, Mom freely volunteered us to perform it for our neighbors as well. Raking leaves and clearing snow, she told us, was part of being a good neighbor.

This lifelong history of helping out made sitting, doing nothing, impossible. Connie kept telling me, "You're so much help with the girls. That's most important." I knew, though, how much time housework took.

I tried lawn-mowing, with the street and driveway as clear boundaries. Surely I could walk in a straight line behind the mower! Connie surveyed my first efforts and announced, "There's no gracious way to tell you, Renay—it'll take me as much time to go around and cut what you missed as if I'd done it myself. Sorry. Maybe we could hire the neighbor boy?"

Vacuuming didn't go much better. Somehow a few children's toys always hid themselves under a table or in the shag carpet. An incident with crayons sent the vacuum to the repair shop.

I managed to scrub floors without damaging anything other than myself. The normally simple task turned into hazardous duty—some days I lost track of the number of times my head got ambushed by a partially open drawer or a counter corner I'd forgotten about.

Laundry was a disaster. I couldn't distinguish different fibers by feel. In my first—and only—attempt, I shrunk Connie's favorite jeans and ruined some sweaters at the same time. Big, big mistake. "That was my absolute favorite outfit. How *could* you?" Connie wailed. "From now on, stay away from the laundry."

As her fury tapered off somewhat, I feebly apologized for my blunder, for ruining in so short a time the most perfect pair of jeans she'd ever owned. Connie said, "I know you're trying to help, but I don't think we can *afford* to have you do laundry."

That night, I could tell she was still angry. "Honey, I'm truly sorry about the jeans."

"I know you are. It's just that—well, this wears on me, too," she replied.

"I don't want to be a burden. Are my efforts of any use in the kitchen?"

"*That's* different," she replied. "I'll take any help you can give me with meals. Three times a day, every day. I don't know how you used to do it."

I'd always been the chief chef at the Poirier residence. I think I spent half my childhood—the half that wasn't spent tumbling through the outdoors with Randy—standing on a chair pulled up to the kitchen counter. Mother, with rolled-up sleeves and frequently a smudge of flour on her nose, let us measure, sprinkle, and stir. Before I was in high school, I could whip up a mean batch of spaghetti sauce, turn out a meat loaf with real mashed potatoes, and sear a steak to perfection. Lasagna, though, was a house favorite. Mom had her own recipe, mixing Wisconsin cheeses with the traditional mozzarella and parmesan.

Cooking without seeing was an adventure every second. At first, even heating up a can of soup for the girls seemed as complicated as a thousand-piece jigsaw puzzle. I had to select the right can off the shelf, then attach the can opener correctly. Pry off the lid without needing first aid. Turn the correct burner to the right temperature. Simmer the soup until it was hot enough to savor, yet not so hot as to burn Alea's tongue. Ladle the right amount into a bowl and then carry it to the table without spilling or tripping over the cat. For the longest time, I seldom attempted anything more complicated than bologna sandwiches.

Eventually, I grew tired of being a culinary coward. I knew it was time to be bold, even audacious in the kitchen. Only one dish came to mind as I contemplated what to make that all of us would enjoy. A treat for my precious family. Lasagna.

The frozen stuff we'd been eating really didn't deserve the same name as the Poirier family recipe. I would take no shortcuts, not even with the sauce. If it took all day, I was going to make real lasagna.

Fortunately, I started early, getting Alea, then five, to help me assemble the ingredients before she took some quiet time while Kara napped. First, we measured flour and sprinkled yeast into the bread machine, something she and I had done together many times. Then we began the real work.

Planning is the secret to cooking by touch, and I think I lay awake half the night figuring out how I was going to do this. I created spaces on the counter for different steps: meat, onions, and celery by the stove to be sautéed. Cheese by the food processor for grating. Salt, pepper, oregano, garlic powder right by the stockpot. Noodles, how to get just enough water in the pot. I decided to stack them on the counter, spiraled as they would be in the water to keep them from sticking. Then I measured the stack with my fingers— how many knuckles high—and filled the pot with water to that height. The pot went to the back of the stove. I wouldn't need the noodles for a while.

Alea was just beginning to read. "M-m-mushroom starts with 'm' doesn't it, Dad? But this can has a big 'C' on it."

"Whoa, thanks, honey!" I'd almost added carrots to the sauce; maybe they'd have enriched the vegetable bouquet, but I was thankful for Alea's eyes. She questioned me again when I asked her to find tomato paste. "The paste in the craft box goes in lasagna?" she asked.

The sauce turned out to be the easiest step. I'd never used a written recipe, anyway, but simply added different spices as I stirred and tasted. Soon I covered the pot so it could simmer and turned my attention to browning the meat.

Right away, new problems assailed me. The burner got so hot that grease spattered everywhere. I knew because it flew all over my hands and arms. I turned it down, too far down. I couldn't tell if the hamburger was browning at all. I decided to go with a slow but steady approach, finally locating a burner setting that produced a gradual sizzle. It was time to add the vegetables.

The trick to chopping onions and celery was proceeding tediously. One slice with the chef's knife. Set it down. Put the chopped pieces into the frying pan. Inch the remaining pieces forward. Another slow chop with my fingers well out of harm's way. Finally, everything was in the pan.

Next came draining the grease. Even when I could see, I sometimes struggled to keep the meat in the pan while pouring the grease into a milk carton. I searched around for a slotted spoon, thinking I could use it to scoop the meat right into the sauce. I'd deal with the grease when it cooled off.

SKREEK—the smoke alarm sounded. The sauce had boiled over onto the coil burner beneath the pot. Quickly, I opened the kitchen window and turned off all the burners rather than waste time hunting for the right one.

The smoke alarm brought Alea running to the kitchen. "Hi, honey," I called in response to her footsteps. "Get me a towel and Daddy'll fan the smoke out the window."

"Do you need my help?" she asked.

"Always, dear," I replied as she handed me the towel.

With the alarm silent once more, I dared to turn on the burner under the pot of water. "Listen, is that Kara stirring?" Alea asked.

Quickly, I walked toward her bedroom. Sure enough, she was cooing. I stepped inside, rubbed her back for a moment, and felt her little body relax back into slumber. Whew!

Soon, the clanging of the lid told us that the noodle water was boiling. I slipped in the noodles and asked Alea to pull a chair over to the counter by the cheeses. The best way not to jam the food processor was to do small chunks of cheese at a time, then empty the container. Alea let me know when the processor had done its work and the cheese seemed sufficiently shredded, although I handled the machine.

I opened up the breadmaker and gently felt for the top of the loaf. Rising nicely. I stopped to think for a moment. Would the noodles be done? Stuck together? Were they morphing into mush?

Methodically, I turned off the burner and asked Alea to move away while I carried the steaming pot to the sink. If the noodles were still hard, I'd have to boil water in another pot, then add it to the noodles.

"Daddy," I heard from Kara's room. I sprayed cold water on the noodles. I'd let them cool off before checking whether they were done.

At this point, I distinctly remembered that making lasagna had always made me feel as if I needed two sets of eyes and an extra hand. If I created one more problem—dropping a pan or losing track of what was cooking again—the whole process would slide into chaos. If the noodles turned to mush on me, I'd never get the dish into the oven before Connie arrived home, and I so wanted to surprise her.

But the noodles were done, although a few had congealed. Alea played with Kara in the living room while I layered sauce, noodles, and cheese into the pan. I slid the heavy dish into the oven, turned it on, and then sat down by the girls. I didn't realize how tired I was until my feet were up on the ottoman. My mind journeyed back through the afternoon. Had I forgotten anything? Did the meat cook all the way through? What if it tasted terrible? My family deserved perfect lasagna, not my experiments.

Soon, though, the tantalizing aromas of baking bread and melting cheeses and bubbling tomato sauce wafted through the house. That's when Connie walked in. "Oh, it smells delightful in here," she said as she gave me a hug.

"Daddy used smoke to make lasagna," Alea announced.

I heard Connie gasp as she turned into the kitchen, and I knew why at once. While I'd tried to keep the mess to a minimum, I'd used just about every pot and bowl we owned in my efforts to stay organized and measure well.

I followed behind Connie. "What can I do to help?"

"Stay put for a second while I clean up the spills on the floor." I believe there was a hint of tears in her voice, but she didn't complain.

I added my elbow grease to Connie's eyesight. Even by feel, I could tell that the tomato sauce mess that had set off the smoke alarm had ruined the catch pan under the stove burner.

Connie took over testing the lasagna for doneness. When we at last sat down and took our first bites, I was back to feeling pretty good, even perhaps elated, about my endeavor. "It's good," my wife said between mouthfuls, "but we've got to make the kitchen easier for you to use."

My confidence increased as I learned how to make the kitchen work for me. The timer on the microwave became a dear friend, loudly proclaiming when my latest creation was done. Connie found some huge kitchen mitts that protected me from spattering grease (I actually went through several pairs). We installed a stronger fan to tame the smoke alarm. And after I ruined about eight coil units/catch pans/rims, Connie presented me with a glass-top stove, cleanable with just a swipe of a rag.

There were a few more disasters: the chicken on the roasting rack that tipped over, spilling grease everywhere. Steaks parched to shoe leather from too much heat. A meat loaf to which I forgot to add the most essential ingredient, the ketchup.

But at long last I reclaimed my position as master chef. That day, I whisked butter, eggs, milk, and my "secret"

I ONCE WAS BLIND

ingredient, vanilla, in only one bowl. I crisped bacon, then used the same pan to fry the griddle cakes. I used a timer for the first set, ninety seconds each side. I flipped them off, tossed one between my hands to cool it off, then took a bite. The slight crunch let me know it was a perfect, golden brown.

Quickly, I fried one large pancake and two small ones for each of my girls, added grapes for the eyes, cheese triangles for the nose, and a bacon smile. Both Kara and Alea exclaimed "Mickey Mouse!" as I placed their plates in front of them, letting me know I'd successfully recreated a restaurant meal they'd once enjoyed.

In reclaiming my former ease in the kitchen, I gleaned an important lesson that stuck with me for our attempts at boating, camping, gardening, and everything else: Keep trying. How could I give up when God never gives up on me?

The courage of our country's forefathers
gave us freedom, along with this truth:
The secret of happiness is freedom,
and the secret of freedom is courage.

8

Sometimes the only way to understand our present path is to walk alongside someone who shared our past.

Uncle Gary

A FEW WEEKS after my ride home ended with helping Josie Johnson, the maintenance manager pushed papers into my hand and said, "Here's some information on technical school classes over in Wausau." Wausau is a good-sized town about eighty miles east of Eau Claire. "If you could learn to use audible computers, as described here, you'd have a job for life in maintenance or other departments. We always need more computer people."

The warmth in his voice made the idea seem exciting. Although typing wasn't my strong suit, I knew that many visually impaired people were able to write very well that way. Further, the promise of long-term, useful employment was the incentive I needed to pursue new training.

I took a Greyhound bus between Eau Claire and Wausau for a three-day stay. Instructors at Wausau Tech tested my ability on several different pieces of adaptive equipment. They gave excellent instructions, then walked around and worked with us individually. By the end of the classes, they'd helped me find the right fit—using an audiotape system and other aids to master keyboarding, specific programs, and applications. I could do most of the training in my own basement.

When I arrived back home, Connie and I sat down in the living room to go through my mail. "Here's a letter from your manager," she said. "Dear Renay, we regret to inform you. . . ."

My job had been terminated. I squeezed my hands together, trying to keep the hurt and confusion I felt from bubbling into tears.

Connie put her hand on my shoulder. "Now we'll have some time together this summer. Maybe I can help you with the computer training."

I tried to focus on what she was saying. Perhaps this computer training was really the answer, a path to more fulfilling employment. Josie had shown me that I could still be useful. I still had hope, hope in the Lord.

"At least we know I can handle the training—glad I spent that time in Wausau before the letter came," I told her with barely a hint of emotion in my voice.

The next morning I contacted one of my instructors at Wausau. She provided wonderful advice on the type of equipment I should purchase and registered me for audio keyboard training.

Connie helped me pick out an electronic typewriter to practice on. Soon the audiotaped lessons arrived. When I finished a set of tapes, I sent them, along with my assignments, to my instructor in Wausau. As soon as the next set of tapes arrived, I called for instructions. Then, every chance I had, I put on my headphones and worked through the current lesson. If I wasn't changing diapers or stacking blocks, I was typing. Alea loved standing by my chair as my fingers clicked away on the keys; she actually learned most of her alphabet as we talked about what I was doing.

Soon I had a certificate testifying to my proficiency on a keyboard. My doctors again certified that I could do the work. They contacted Cray and I thought I'd be back on the job in a few days.

But it didn't work out that way. While Cray offered me a work order processor position, they didn't have the talking computer I needed. Weeks again turned into months as I waited for a call that my workstation was ready. I wanted to work, not wait.

I struggled to keep my spirits up as self-doubts surfaced over whether I would ever have a real job again. I longed to talk things over with Uncle Gary, my confidante for so many years. Gary lived in Florida now. Phone conversations didn't lend themselves to the kind of heart-to-heart conversation I craved, and I knew I needed someone besides Connie to talk things through with, someone who wasn't so directly affected by my choices and dilemmas. *Talk to Gary, he'll understand*, kept running through my brain. *He's in seminary now . . . he'll help you work through things.*

Gary is just five years older than me. Growing up, our relationship had all the best things about being brothers without the fighting or having to share a room. Uncle Gary, my mother's little brother, lived just a few blocks from us. I was eight, he was thirteen when Mom began renting the house around the corner from her parents, Grandma and Grandpa Meier. Gary never treated Randy and me like pests, but actually seemed to enjoy coming up with things for us to do.

Any idea that Gary had seemed great to Randy and me. A few sticks and a crumpled-up piece of paper for a puck gave us everything we needed for backyard hockey. A table in the basement became a mountain for "Condor," Gary's version of king of the hill. Together we hauled boards, nails, hammers, and saws down to the creek, where Gary helped us build a platform fort halfway up a tree—every boy's dream.

Gary also joined in the neighborhood football games, our summertime obsession. About twenty of us gathered, and if someone was late, we'd head to their homes to see if we could help out with chores so they wouldn't miss the kickoff. I think we played on the biggest field in history, measuring at least 150 yards from end zone to end zone, through a half dozen yards along the creek. A scoring drive could take half the evening, right up until halftime, more commonly known as dinnertime. Unless we had a player shortage, Gary, Randy, and I stuck together on the same side.

Over short distances, Gary was one of the fastest runners in town. His asthma, though, stymied his athletics. Grandma and Grandpa Meier kept a nebulizer at the house for him. Gary poured his athletic hopes into tennis, and even made it to the state tournament, yet he hadn't ever learned to swim—he was allergic to fish, bee stings, and other things that cut down on what he could do outside. While Gary wasn't exactly sickly, he had to know his limits. Still, he often tromped down to the Bloomer beach at Lake Como with us on afternoons when we just wanted to play in the sand.

Gary also mentored me in the fine art of practical jokes. I think it started with escorting friends through the dark, abandoned egg plant across the street from his house. Gary warned them of ghosts and mummies. Then I'd hide in its "secret" passages, just made for jumping out of to scare our victims.

Gary often tugged on a black stocking cap and turned up the collar of his jacket. With his hands in his pockets, he did a good imitation of a street gang member. We told some of the younger boys that it was Gary's twin brother Dean from Chicago. Gary never said a word, just looked at them, and they tore away as fast as they could go.

But the most effective prank we pulled was born of a moment. One afternoon, a record number of ducks crowded the creek below Grandpa's house, looking, well, like sitting ducks. Gary said, "They're not moving. I wonder if we could catch one."

We pulled a couple of fishing nets out of Grandpa's garage and quietly made our way down the embankment. At Gary's signal, I dropped my net over the closest bird. Success!

I looked over. Gary had one, too. He motioned for me to head up the bank. "I've got an idea," he said. "Let's put them in the garage."

"Why?"

"Let's see how many we can get before Dad gets home." I saw the possibilities. I was game for it. After all, it was his dad's garage. I wondered, too, how many we'd capture before the rest of the flock flew away.

Gary and I each made at least thirty-five trips from the creek to the garage, our nets full. With suppertime fast approaching, we quit catching and hid in the bushes to see what would happen. I remember thinking that the garage was amazingly quiet for having half a gross of birds inside.

Soon Grandpa's car turned into the driveway. No push-button openers in those days; Grandpa eased out of the car, reached down for the garage door handle, pulled it up—and just about lost his balance as seventy ducks quacked and swirled around their liberator.

Was Grandpa upset? Not really, he joined in our laughter for a bit. Then he said, "Dinner'll keep while you two gather buckets and scrub brushes to clean up after your feathered friends." Yes, the joke was on us, especially since Grandpa decided we might as well hose out the whole garage. It took hours. It also curbed our appetite for pranks for awhile.

When we got older, Gary wasn't always so willing to head to the beach with us. "I feel like a fool, just wading while the rest of you swim," he confided to me.

"I can teach you to swim," I said with the kind of confidence only twelve-year-olds have.

Gary looked at me for a moment, then shrugged. "What have I got to lose?"

We headed over to the beach. I recognized the lifeguard, so I went over to his chair and told him my plans. He chuckled, "Okay, go ahead."

I waded out to the safety line that stretched out from the dock, where the water was about four feet deep. Gary said, "It's too shallow there. I feel dumb enough not being able to swim. I don't want to be in the baby area."

He walked out to the end of the dock and sat down, kicking his feet through the water for a while. The ripples spread out across the calm, clear lake, finally reaching where I stood. Before I could suggest another way to start, Gary murmured, "Well, here I go," and jumped in.

He sank to the bottom like a block of concrete. I could see his arms reaching toward the surface as he tried to scratch his way above the water. As fast as I could, I swam toward him, knowing the water was over my head as well, then dove down toward his feet rather than risk having him clutch at me.

I grabbed Gary by the legs, using the natural buoyancy of water to walk him toward the safety line. In moments his face was above water again; he coughed and sputtered. Later, he told me, "It seemed pitch-black under the water, even though I could see the glimmer of sunlight on the waves when I looked up. I almost panicked, cut off from everything, when I felt you grab my legs and walk me toward safety. Uh, thanks."

Several weeks passed before I talked Gary into trying again. This time, he stayed inside the rope area. By the end of the summer, he had a pretty good dog paddle, flutter kick, and back float. He could swim.

Before long, Gary was off earning a two-year lab tech degree and I was busy playing high-school football. By the time he left Bloomer for his first job, my time was taken up as starting quarterback. But Gary came home every weekend; we still had time for drives in Gary's Ford LTD, listening to eight-track tapes. Or we'd pick up a pizza from Sammy's, Gary's favorite, then drive north of town to Round Lake and toss a Frisbee around.

We never lost touch with each other. Gary married and had three children before Connie became my wife. Then he decided to enroll in Bible college. In 1990, Gary and his family moved to Clearwater, Florida, for his schooling. He confided, "I always wanted to be a chemistry teacher, but I knew Dad couldn't afford to send me to a four-year school. This is my chance to be a teacher in another way."

Gary's sister Bonnie called him right away with the news of my accident. He later told me, "Renay, hearing that news sucked the air right out of my lungs, as if a bomb had gone off next to me."

In the year following the accident, Gary and I talked by phone, but I often wished he still lived in Marshfield, only an hour's drive, for good conversation. Gary had had to give up on dreams, too. I couldn't talk about the emptiness, the uselessness I felt, over the phone. Yes, I could share anything with Connie, and I'd also had some helpful conversations with Father Menzel, but that wasn't the same as working things through with another husband, a father, who had known me literally my whole life, who was a soulmate.

Finally, Connie and I agreed that I should head to Florida for a visit. I think Connie sensed the depth of my depression as the months went by without my finding significant employment. For me, I felt drawn by a yearning for someone who shared memories of nothing but good times with me— ducks and pizza and an era where evenings meant football and danger meant trying to shimmy eighty feet to the top of Bloomer's curfew siren tower. I wasn't running away, but rather searching for something that was gone.

Something else drove me to Florida as well, a need to face my fears. Still without meaningful work, the future seemed more like a place of nightmares than of dreams. I knew that Connie had fears of her own; I needed to work through mine with someone else. Looking back, given how I was still avoiding going out in public at that time, uncertain of how to get around or how to interact with others, I'm amazed that I got on the plane.

But I hadn't been with Gary for years and the thought of being with him propelled me forward. The day before I left, I called Sammy's Pizza. Was there a way to pack a couple of pizzas topped with hamburger, mushrooms, onions, and extra cheese to carry with me to Florida? They assured me that frozen pizzas could survive the trip.

Then I called Gary to make the final arrangements and said, "Tell Lynn that I'm cooking dinner. Honest. Don't let her prepare anything."

Memories of the week I spent with Gary blur into a collection of walks on the beaches, sitting in the sand while the water splashed over my feet, Lynn's cry of "Oh, Gary's going to be so happy!" when I pulled out the Sammy's Pizza boxes, and long, long conversations about Bloomer, about life, and about God.

Gary, then a senior in Bible college, was taking a wisdom literature class, the central focus of which was Job and his sufferings. "Crazy, isn't it," he said, "that something written thousands of years ago can still be relevant today."

"Crazy, isn't it," I murmured back, "that you'd be studying it just as I needed to hear this so much."

Listening to the sea gulls and breaking waves, we hashed over the big questions. Why do bad things happen to good people? What was I supposed to do now with my life? Who would protect my girls? How could I keep from being a burden on others? Why, when I so wanted to work, couldn't I find something to do?

Not that we only studied the Bible that week; we picnicked with his family and walked every beach near his home. But by the third or fourth day of my visit, the week seemed less like a vacation and more like a spiritual journey.

Saturday night, my last evening with Gary and Lynn, we stayed up past midnight, conversing and eating pizza from a local shop that was almost as tasty as Sammy's. As we called it a night, Gary said, "I wonder if we'll wake up in time for church. We've been attending a new place, kind of a community church."

"Let's just see," I replied. Secretly, I hoped we wouldn't go. All too often I managed to trip on something in a strange place. Instead, I hoped for one last walk on the wide-open beaches where I felt free to take long strides.

But the next morning I awoke early, rested and refreshed. I could hear someone rattling dishes around in the kitchen. It was Gary. In no time, all six of us were packed in the car and on our way. The church was so new to Gary and Lynn that they hadn't met the pastor yet.

From the moment we stepped through the doors of the building, I felt its warmth and friendliness. Hanging on to Gary's shoulder as I was, everyone certainly knew I was a stranger, but the "Good morning" greetings that circled around us seemed to have just the right note of cheer in them. Suddenly, I felt good.

I ONCE WAS BLIND

Gary led me to a pew and his family sat down on the other side of me. As the organist played soft yet upbeat music, Gary described the sanctuary to me. "There's a platform up front, and the minister is already seated on a chair there, smiling as people come in. The children are all gathered on one side for the opening prayers, then they'll go off for Sunday school."

The music tapered off and the pastor asked for prayer requests. People shouted out concerns and praises from everywhere in the sanctuary. The children said a few prayers in unison before they left.

After another song, the pastor began his announcements with, "I actually prepared two sermons and was up half the night trying to decide which one to deliver today. But I feel like I was guided this morning to speak about the blind man."

The hair stood up on the back of my neck. Goosebumps formed all over my body as Gary clutched my leg, saying, "Oh my God, Renay." I had no doubt that God was speaking to me.

The minister read from the story of Bartimaeus. Then he painted a word picture of the poor beggar ignored by the crowds who were straining to catch a glimpse of Jesus.

Bartimaeus had never seen the lilies of the field
that Jesus described,
or the golden temple roof that glistened
above the streets of Jerusalem,
or the smiles of those who reached out a hand
to help a stranger.
But he wasn't the only one who was blind.
People walked right past Bartimaeus without
seeing him, without knowing who he was.
Instead of helping him, they told him to hush.

He was a nuisance to them, not a man. They were
just as blind as he was. And so are all of us.
Close your eyes for a moment. Imagine you've lost
your sight. What would you do?
Could you keep your job, your friends?
Could you even leave this room without a guide,
without someone to lean on?
Open your eyes again, but remember
that in some way all of us are blind.
Perhaps we've failed to understand
the needs of someone we love.
Or we don't believe we've been given talents
and gifts by God.
Or we ignored chances to be the hands of Jesus
to another.
Or we don't want to search for what God
has in mind for us.
Perhaps Bartimaeus was actually the most blessed
of all who lined the dusty road from Jericho
that day, for he knew what he needed:
Mercy.
And in his darkness he knew who
could answer his prayer:
Jesus.
Others along the road that day told Bartimaeus to
be quiet, for they didn't understand that Jesus is
looking for those of us who are in darkness,
who need the light that he alone can bring.
Even with 20/20 eyesight, we can be blind
to the fact that Jesus,
and Jesus alone,
can show us where we need to go
and who we are to become.
Let us all look to Jesus and Jesus alone.

AS THE MINISTER closed with prayer, the love of God seemed to flow through me. I still had no idea what the future held for me, but a new hope began to push away the stabs of fear that had lived in my heart for so long. *Yes, Jesus, I prayed, I can go on now. I still have questions but I'm not afraid to ask them anymore. I know you're with me. I know you'll show me the way.*

Later, as Gary drove me to the airport, I confided, "This trip was a lifesaver. I needed to get away, to get a fresh perspective. All of your wisdom readied me to hear the minister's message today."

Gary said, "Hey, you saved me once, you know. I'll never forget being under the murky waters of good old Lake Como, unable to reach the light, then feeling you grasp my legs and push me toward the sunshine."

"Well, now you've carried me. Thanks."

"Gosh, what are uncles for?"

*It is only through each other
that we move on to better things.*

9

Admitting we need help is often the biggest, most difficult step toward getting that assistance.

Helping Hands

"I KNOW where the pizza counter is," I told Connie. "Just drop me off right in front of the door and I can find my way down one hallway." Connie and I had several errands to run and I didn't want to slow her down.

After a moment's hesitation, Connie replied, "Okay, but wait right inside the door with the pizza. I'll hop out of the car when I get back."

Slowly, I opened the car door and stepped out onto the curb. The sidewalk would be five, six steps across . . . there was the door, I was inside. I reached out with my right hand to find the wall and followed it down the hallway. This wasn't so tough. I didn't always need someone else to guide me. There were so many things I *couldn't* do on my own— like notice when I'd spilled something on my shirt, or drive to the store for an extra carton of milk—that I desperately searched for things I could do without help.

I heard a gasp. Then a woman muttered, "Look at that drunk over there. Stay by me, honey."

A child's voice replied, "Is he really drunk, Mommy?" They were talking about *me*. I tried to picture what they saw, a man shuffling his feet, staggering along a wall. Is that what I looked like? Instead of being independent, I was a spectacle. I needed help. *Rehabilitation. A cane.*

For months I'd avoided rehabilitation because the doctors had assured me that my sight would return. Using a cane seemed pointless. A cane wouldn't help me see my girls or let me drive a car. Would a thin rod of fiberglass help me be of use to anyone or would it simply advertise my lack of vision? Someone had suggested a guide dog; but who would clean up after it? Connie didn't need any more burdens.

I called Dr. Redman's office. The office manager told me, "The best place is the Society for the Blind in Minneapolis. . . . No, I'm not sure how long the training lasts. . . . I don't have any specific information on what they can teach you. Here's their phone number."

Each phone call seemed to raise more questions than it answered, but the offer of better employment at Cray was the catalyst I needed to enroll in training. After nine months of keyboard practice and negotiation with Cray, the maintenance department finally procured a talking computer and I started my job as a work order processor. Right away, Cray sent me for a weeklong training session at the Minnesota Society for the Blind to learn to use a specific program called VERT Plus.

At the start of my first class the instructor announced, "Learning this program is a monthlong process." *Great*, I thought. *And I've got a week. Guess I'll make the best of it— as if we ever know how much time we have, anyway!*

While my keyboarding was quite proficient, computers themselves were still mysteries to me. "Press any button you can touch and the computer will talk to you," the instructor reassured me. "You can't hurt the computer."

Hesitantly, I tapped one finger. A squeaky voice said, "E."

"Immediate feedback. Great," I said. A half-hour later as I confidently typed up a storm, the machine suddenly went quiet.

"Hey," someone next to me said. Her computer was down, too—the whole network was. Eventually, they traced the problem back to my machine.

"I told you," I admitted, "that if there's a way to mess up on a computer, I can find it."

Other than that incident, the training went fairly well. After computer sessions, I took advantage of other classes on cooking, getting organized, and using a cane.

I learned about Hi-Mark, a simple tube of quick-drying gel that I used to label our stove at home, our TV, and equipment at work. We tried Scriptwriters, clipboards with a guiding wire that clicked down the page so you could avoid writing over other lines. The instructor passed around all kinds of storage bins and marking tools that could be used to stay organized. And we learned to use a cane.

My cane had four separate sections, strung together with a shock cord like some tent rods are. A few quick finger movements and the sections snapped into place. The instructors taught us how to hold it, how to move it back and forth to feel for things, and sent us out into the hall to practice.

I concentrated on walking steadily, although slowly, trying to let the cane guide me, when *Whoomph!* Something fell in front of me. I knelt down—a woman just coming out of a classroom had tripped over my cane. She wasn't hurt, but I felt just terrible. How many people would I trip with this thing? The instructor reminded all of us that in the real world the people around us could see our canes.

Eventually, we ventured outside, working our way around obstacles and following simple directions. Using a cane saved my shins and knees. For months after the accident, I probably had the worst looking legs in the world, scraped and bruised from running into things. Not only did the cane protect my shins, but it gave me more and more freedom, the more adept I became at using it. As my confidence grew, I pictured myself as Luke Skywalker, my cane a light saber, arming me to fight against the darkness.

I think I reached Jedi Master status one early winter morning. Our instructor announced, "It's time for each of you to tackle a solo adventure. I'll be watching from here while you each move toward a destination I assign to you. Ready or not, here you go. Renay, you're off to the luncheon grille we visited yesterday. Charlotte. . . ."

I barely heard the other students' assignments as I tried to remember the exact location of the restaurant. Determined, I headed down the sidewalk toward the first intersection. A few cars swished by, letting me know that the few inches of snow that had fallen the night before were melting into splashing puddles. My cane found the curb and I turned to cross the main street. Pausing, I listened hard for cars, then stepped out into the street—and into ankle-deep, icy slush. Feeling every bit the fearless explorer, I forged ahead, my cane leading the way. Tap, tap . . . the curb! Up on dry land once again, a left turn, and Eureka! The restaurant door! Steaming hot chocolate with extra whipped cream was the perfect celebration.

I learned to navigate my way into a store, then ask for directions to the front desk or to customer service. With the cane, I'd be able to take Alea and Kara Christmas shopping while Connie ran other errands.

The rehabilitation classes helped immensely, but it was a little bit like winning a year's supply of ice cream without having a freezer to store it in. I still needed help—I knew how to negotiate crossing the street with my cane, yet someone had to give me excellent directions before that cane did me any good.

Even careful planning wasn't always enough. I walked the same path every day across the University of Eau Claire campus for a summer-school class. My cane found the sidewalk intersections that would direct me to the right building and—one afternoon the concrete disappeared under my feet! In an instant I fell straight down, tumbling to the bottom of a six-foot-deep trench. The jolt took my breath away, my hands and feet were numb, my chest tight from fearing where I was. I felt for my cane, then ran my hands against the dirt walls of the trench, trying to find a foothold. But to where, where was I going? Direction had escaped me completely. Just as I felt my blood pressure rising from panic, a voice said, "Hey, are you all right?"

"Yeah I think so. No treasure down here," I replied as I felt his strong hand reach down for mine.

"I was cutting grass across the way when I spotted you— they're doing utility repairs along here today. I screamed with all my might. I'm so sorry, I was just too far away and my tractor wouldn't go any faster. Then you disappeared. My God, I was afraid of what I might see when I got over here," he said. I crawled back on to the sidewalk and stood with his assistance.

Despite shooting pains that had me wondering if anything was broken, I said, "Well, honestly, only my dignity is smarting," giving what was probably a lame smile. I couldn't help wondering how long I might have been stuck in that trench if he hadn't seen me. *Isn't that what happens, though?* a voice inside my head seemed to say. *Someone is always there just as you need them to point you in the right direction.*

The jolt of falling into that trench set my thinking straight. I couldn't completely avoid having crazy things like that happen unless I wanted to stay closed up in my home. I couldn't afford to be trapped by fears of making a fool of myself or of failing to reach my destinations; I had to expand my horizons. I took to heart that it's not what happens to you, but what you do about it, that matters.

Life is full of laughter, humor, excitement, adventure,
even in a simple breath of fresh morning air.
It's the best air we have to breath.
Plunge into the sea of life,
teeming with love, and smile.

10

The human spirit is both fragile and resilient. Looking back, I sometimes feel guilty that it took me so long to once and for all place my future in God's hands, yet the wounds to my spirit were deep. God is sovereign, I am not. I am in no position to question our Lord's ways.

Only when I traveled to the darkest place that the soul can journey did this truth come alive for me.

The Very Bottom

AN OFFICE with a window to slide open for a breeze. My very own L-shaped desk and computer. A swivel chair. An in-basket full of maintenance requests, real work that I was qualified to handle. More than a year and a half after the accident, I was finally back at work.

My job was straightforward but vital. The talking computer let me understand the maintenance requests that employees submitted. Then, with my knowledge of the work, I briefed the technicians on what needed to be done. In effect, I was a middleman, a troubleshooter, able to partially diagnose the problem and send the right crew with the right equipment.

In a way, the position was a custom fit for me, still allowing me to use my electrical knowledge. The hardest thing to get used to was sitting behind a desk rather than being out and about, doing the repairs myself. Yet I appreciated having my own desk, my own little office that proved to me that once again, I'd found a place.

After just three months, my manager called me aside and said, "I've got a productivity report in front of me. The technicians are getting a lot more done these days, mostly because you can anticipate who and what is needed to do the job. Keep up the good work."

Even though I longed to be part of the crew, my coworkers elected me as their safety representative. That gave me more contact with people. While Cray certainly followed safety procedures, we had some issues around air/water quality, noise levels, and inadequate procedures for working in both electrical and confined spaces. My coworkers thought that management was more willing to listen to me, given my accident.

At my first performance review, my manager confirmed that my efforts were increasing efficiencies for the whole department. "You're doing a great job and you need to know that the men respect you," he said in closing as he pounded me on the back. "As safety rep, though, I'm not sure you always know who's in the room for meetings. Be careful who you lock horns with."

I shrugged and said, "The issues are real; the men count on me to speak up."

"You're right, just be careful who you rile up." I remember walking out with a sense of self-confidence. I was again making the most of what I could do.

So I wasn't prepared, not at all prepared, for what happened the week after my review. October 21, 1993. I'd actually gotten to work a bit early and was at my computer when my manager asked me to attend a meeting in a few minutes. I finished up the report I was working on, then grabbed my cane and felt my way along the corridor to the conference room.

Before I could find a chair, someone said, "As of this morning, we no longer have a position for you. It's been eliminated."

I felt like I'd been sucker-punched, then kicked in the stomach. "What? Why?"

"It's just one of those things, for the best, I'm sure." He told me that a taxi was already waiting to take me home. "Someone will box up your personal things and we'll ship them to you."

A security guard joined my manager and supervisor in escorting me to a cab that was waiting by the front door. "Sorry," my manager muttered, "but all of this is for your own good." My mind couldn't take in what he was saying. Shock and bewilderment pared down my thoughts to, *You're being escorted out of the building as if you'd committed some crime.* The cab driver opened the back door for me and I stumbled into the darkness of the cab.

In less than an instant, I'd been plunged from hope back into despair. *Why, God? I had mastered the work. I can't bear to think of sitting home, alone, useless again. What do I do now?*

The cab driver seemed to know better than to say anything. I cracked a window, hoping that fresh air would ease the lump in my throat and I'd be able to take a deep breath again, but it didn't help. Sitting in the darkness, I couldn't see a future; only empty minutes and days stretched ahead of me.

The cab halted. From the whizzing of cars in front of us, I assumed we were at a stoplight. I decided I couldn't go home, not yet. I couldn't tell Connie the news. So, without warning, I opened the cab door and stumbled out.

I had no idea where I was and I didn't care. I could tell by the shadows and lack of traffic that I was in a neighborhood of small homes, one of the older parts of town. I stumbled into a fence. I gave it a shake, angry that it stopped me, and thought, *No, you won't stop me.* I climbed over it, dropping to the ground.

For at least an hour I wandered that way, stumbling along, half-hoping that a car might hit me. Then I wouldn't have to think anymore. The words of Connie's friend echoed in my ear, *Caring for Renay must be like having a third child.* That's all I was to Connie, a burden. When I heard the roar of the river, I knew what I had to do. The frigid October waters would make it easy to slip away. I'd give Connie the chance to start over.

I walked toward the sound of the river, knowing it was far below where I stood, down a steep, overgrown embankment. I stumbled into the guardrail, climbed over it, and the ground fell away.

I slipped and tumbled over rocks and thorn bushes until my fall was broken by a small tree. If I crawled, maybe I'd be able to find a path to the water. My only thought was ending it all, for what use was I to anyone? Then the brush stopped. I felt the roughness of gravel and I knew where I was, on the gravel path that led to the old Chicago & Northwestern railroad bridge. I could climb out on the bridge which towered a hundred feet above the waters, then jump from there. Quickly, I crawled across the gravel, searching for the steel rails. All I had to do was follow them out onto the bridge. Crouching now, the steel between my fingers, I moved as fast as I could.

But suddenly, there was nothing to hold onto. I reached out only to feel air. Where were the trestles? Later I learned that a fire just three months before had taken out the center span of the bridge, but at the time, I could only think, *I've failed again. I can't even kill myself.*

I listened to the roar of the river, trying to remember if the bank below the bridge was clear enough for me to make it to the water, when a voice spoke to me, *Renay, that was a wonderful thing you did for me.* Even though I'd never heard her speak, I knew it was Josie Johnson. *You can help others. . . .*

I shivered, then started shaking as I sat down right where I was. What was I doing? I pictured Connie's smile, remembered the feel of Kara's hand pulling me toward our swings, Alea kissing my eyes and saying, "Don't worry, Daddy, God will take care of you." How could I doubt that my girls needed me, whether or not my company did?

I made my way back over the trestles, praying, *God, I can't find my way alone, not back home, not to what you want me to do. Please show me.*

Eventually the gravel path crossed the roadway. I stood at the curb, knowing that between the holes in my clothing and scratches all over from the rocks and brambles, I had to look like a wild man. As I tried to gather my thoughts enough to know which direction led home, a car slowed, then stopped. A man asked if I needed a ride.

I asked for a lift to the nursing home where my mother was employed. I had to talk with someone else before I faced Connie.

As soon as Mom saw me, she knew that something was terribly wrong. For two hours she let me talk. I spilled everything that had spiraled me down into despair.

"Renay," she said gently, "the catastrophe you face isn't being blind. It's your lack of vision of the future. You're a father, with two wonderful girls. That's work right there. But God has more for you to do. I think this time it will be with people. I know God's got work for you to do."

With that, she offered to drive me home.

I didn't need to say much to Connie; my few words told her enough for us to hold each other tight. After supper, bath time, and bedtime for the girls, she and I sat down on the couch together. Connie leaned her head against my shoulder and I put my arms around her.

"Darkness and gloom just about had their way with me today," I whispered. "Lost, that's what I was, like the poor little lamb Jesus spoke of. Away from the flock, off in the wilderness."

"Jesus said the shepherd would go after the one stray lamb, just as God stopped you today," she whispered back.

I pondered her words, then gave voice to my prayer. "Lord, you are my God, my shepherd. There is no other refuge."

Maybe I had to hit rock bottom and contemplate bringing my life to an end before I could start over. Up until then, I think I was still trying to create a new future on my own. But my thinking had brought me to the railroad trestles, a crossroad where I tried to take the future into my own hands.

From then on, my prayers shifted. I knew God had allowed me to hear Josie's voice. It was time to leave everything behind from my life as an electrician. Putting my hope in the Lord, I began searching for a brand-new career. And I prayed, *God, show me how I can help others. Please.*

Without God, I am only part of who I could be,
weak and frail, cautious and unsure.
Yet, guided by the hand of Love,
I feel God's presence and smile
for all to see.

11

Fears of an empty future, despair at not being able to see the faces of my family, ruled my life until the voice of Josie Johnson called to me by the river. Misery blinded me to all the other prayers God had been answering and all the blessings that surrounded me: my wife, my children, the rest of my family, the friends who stood by me.

This blindness to the love all around me was far darker than my physical blindness—and far less easy to explain, for life's lessons had given me better instruction than that.

Finding the Light

I COULDN'T HAVE been more than seven years old; we had just moved into a little rental house a few blocks from Grandpa Meier's home in Bloomer. The coolness of the morning air woke me before dawn and I crawled out of bed toward the foot-square floor vent through which heat from the oil-burning stove, which took up a good chunk of the first-floor living room, wafted toward me.

Through the vent, I could see my mother in the kitchen, pulling out pans and energetically wielding the eggbeater. A mixed aroma of fruit and spice filled the air—apple pie for dinner!

She'd turned on the radio and every so often talked back to it, longing for conversation while her children slept on.

Softly, I tiptoed downstairs to join her. She started singing softly along with an old dance tune. Peeking around the corner of the kitchen, I saw her break into a little jig, oblivious of the flour that coated her hands and face. Then suddenly she stopped, hung her head, and murmured, "I miss you so." With a sigh, she made her way slowly back to the stove.

My mother, lonely and sad—it was a revelation to me, for she made her five children feel like the center of her universe. She'd turned each of our little abodes into welcoming homes: the house without running water on her in-laws' farm, the second-floor apartment in Bloomer, and now this tiny house with a bedroom for the boys, one for the girls, and a bath to share.

"We're a family, we work together and play together," was Mom's wisdom to us, whether our larder was down to nothing but lettuce and mayo sandwiches or full from canning beans, tomatoes, and beets from our garden. She wasn't more than twenty-four herself, living on wisps of income while trying to raise five children under the age of seven. The small wages from any regular employment her high-school diploma could bring her wouldn't cover day care.

I knew we were different from the other families in town because we didn't have a dad, but Mom taught us that we were a complete family, bound together in love. "We just need to stay together and be strong," she told us, both in word and deed.

As I grew older and started to grasp the tremendous burdens Mom carried, I finally appreciated her joyful spirit. She'd chosen to rejoice in all circumstances.

Then Mom remarried, gave us a new baby brother named John, and moved to a brand-new home outside of town. I had my high-school diploma; it was time to strike out on my own. At eighteen, I found steady employment with J. H. Larson and moved into my own apartment in Eau Claire. I didn't have to share a room or the TV with anyone. Working over forty hours a week left little time for stopping home to visit Mom or my sisters. Sometimes Mom would hint, "John so enjoys it when you play catch or hide-and-seek with him."

"They scheduled me to work Saturday, Mom. Sorry." Now that I was an adult, I didn't see a need to stay together.

Randy, now in the Air Force, often stayed with me when he was home on leave. Sometimes I teased him, "Guess I'd better drop you off for your mandatory talk with Mom. Gotta do that once a month, you know."

One phone call, a single conversation that stopped time, changed everything. Mom's voice quavered as she said, "It's Kim, and little John, and Grandpa John. The Jeep flipped, they're all in the hospital. Can you meet me there?"

Randy and I clocked probably a hundred miles an hour along the road to the Bloomer hospital, but by the time we arrived, only Grandpa John was there, still unconscious. Kim and John had been taken to Sacred Heart Hospital in Eau Claire.

Driving the same roads once again, waves of fear crashed through Randy and me. Kim and John, how could their lives be in danger, all because of a motorist who'd lost control while passing another car?

It had all happened so quickly. Grandpa John, my mother's new father-in-law, helped out each day by picking up little John from the babysitter and Kim from middle school. That afternoon, Kim had helped Grandpa carry the extra diapers and bottles from the sitter, then climbed into the passenger seat of the Jeep with two-year-old John (this was in the 1970s, before car seats were popular).

As Grandpa was turning into my mother's driveway, another car, oblivious of him, had moved into his lane to pass and broadsided the Jeep so hard that it flew fifteen feet into the air, getting caught in the branches of a huge oak tree.

Kim had seen the car just in time to curl herself around John, but after hanging for a moment, the two of them fell to the ground. Her ribs broken, one puncturing her lung, my little sister pulled herself arm over arm toward the side door.

Shanon, hearing the screeching tires and crash, flew out the garage door and found Kim and John. She half-dragged, half-carried Kim and little John into the house, where Kim lost consciousness. Shanon called 911, then my mother. Mom kept her on the phone until the ambulance arrived, trying to calm her.

When Randy and I arrived at Sacred Heart, Mom was sitting beside Kim, eyes full of tears. My heart, which hadn't stopped pounding since my phone rang, pounded even harder at the sight of Kim, unconscious, hooked up to tubes and machines. Kim, my football-playing buddy, hurt so badly. John was doing fine, they said.

That night, Grandpa John regained consciousness long enough to ask Mom, "The little ones, are they all right?" Assured that Kim and John were okay, he closed his eyes again, and passed away a short time later. That night, the rest of us gathered at Grandpa and Grandma Meier's home. No one wanted to be alone, least of all me.

Grandpa John's death cast a shadow over all of us, but as we thought of the Jeep, still in the tree, or of Kim struggling to breathe, even though we knew her lung would heal, our fingers reached out to each other. Hands grasped, words of thankfulness spilled over. "We're still a family. I'm sorry I haven't called you more. I'll never forget again how much all of you mean to me."

YET I *HAD* forgotten the lessons I'd learned: the treasure of a loving family, worth more than any other gifts, certainly more than my sight; and Mom's impeccable modeling of rejoicing in spite of what happens to us. By the morning of October 9, 1990, as I stood in my little palace of a home thanking God for all my blessings, the age-old trap of believing that our lives were somehow charmed, that our struggles were over, had ensnared me. God's love was the only guarantee in life:

Again I saw under the sun
that the race is not won by the swift,
nor the battle by the valiant,
nor a livelihood by the wise,
nor riches by the shrewd,
nor favor by the experts;
for a time of calamity comes to all alike.
(Ecclesiastes 9:11)

Okay, God, I prayed, let the miracle of my family's love for each other help me to rejoice, no matter what my future holds. Let me concentrate on your light, whatever my circumstances may be. I also prayed for a new kind of self-worth, fed by understanding the gifts God had given me rather than by my work or my job.

Still, every evening Connie and I prayed for my eyesight to be restored. Jesus encouraged us to be persistent in prayer. He told his disciples of a widow who pleaded again and again with the town judge, saying, "Grant me justice against my adversary." Eventually, the judge ruled in her favor rather than be bothered anymore (Luke 18:1–8).

So I continued to pray for a miracle for my eyes, but only after I'd praised God for each blessing that came my way.

Our faith so slowly grows, through God's love and faith and patience, until finally, we begin to reach toward heaven...

12

"You can help others . . . work with people . . . God has work for you to do. . . ." As I worked to pull myself back together after nearly ending it all, I focused on my mother's words, on the words I thought I'd heard Josie Johnson say. I needed to be out in the world helping others.

Finding a New Place

SOUNDS FROM THE BREWERS baseball game on television filled the living room, making me feel not quite so alone. Connie was at work, the girls at the sitter. Absent-mindedly, I ran a brush through Punkin's fur. "You must be tired of my company, buddy," I whispered to our cat.

Those months after losing the work order processing job seemed darker than those right after my accident. For weeks, I cocooned at home, unable to focus enough to plan for the future. I continued going to church and to physical therapy for my ongoing neck and back problems, but otherwise I avoided seeing people outside of my immediate family. I had nothing to say. Who else would hire me? Was I employable or a liability to my family?

Eventually, I contacted Wisconsin's Department of Vocational Rehabilitation (DVR), a place I'd never heard of before losing my sight. "You're still on Cray's payroll. We can't provide services," a counselor told me.

"I don't want disability pay," I said. "I want to find another job." I'd already proved I could still work.

Finally, the counselor suggested a series of assessment tests, "to see how well you can function in employment and in the community. I need those results before I can provide any training funds."

For two days, I worked through manual dexterity tests, aptitude tests, tests to see if I could remember where I placed things in order to pick them up again. All the results were shipped back to the DVR. The counselor called me for an appointment. "Can't we talk over the phone?" I asked. "Transportation is a problem."

"I can only counsel in person," she said adamantly. So I called friends to procure a ride.

Once there, she devoted about forty-five minutes to filling out forms and gathering information that I'd already submitted. Then, as our session drew to a close, she said, "Well, I've matched your skills to the jobs I'm aware of. Two would allow you to begin right away."

I leaned forward in anticipation, then slumped a bit as she said, "One of the fast food restaurants in town has worked with the visually impaired before and would hire you as a fry cook. Or, there's a battery factory in River Falls that could accommodate you on their assembly line."

Burgers or batteries, hot grease or acid, I said, "But I've already shown that I can work with computers. And we can't move."

"I'm out of time. Let me know what you decide," she said as she ushered me out the door.

That was my introduction to the DVR system. Perhaps if I'd first sought counseling for my depression, I could have navigated the system more successfully. Psychologically I was a mess, with nightmares of the accident, of losing my job, of being unable to protect my family, all robbing me of sleep. In the job search process, I was trying to grasp for straws that I couldn't seem to find. I wanted direction and instead I hit barriers.

I know that the DVR provides wonderful services to many people, but somehow I got caught in a part of the system that had broken down. Whether due to limited funding, burned-out personnel, or outmoded rules, no one seemed to be able to help me explore other meaningful work possibilities.

Part of the problem was me, I'm sure. I didn't understand the rules. I wanted answers; they asked me to wait. I knew I needed training; they thought I should wait. I grew tired of making yet another appointment, only to hear the counselor tell me to wait some more.

One afternoon during a physical therapy session, an idea wedged its way into my thoughts. My sessions with Joan, Josie's granddaughter, had helped me so much. I wondered, "Joan, have you heard of any visually impaired physical therapists?"

"I don't know any personally, but I believe one graduated a class or two ahead of me," she answered.

"How much of your job requires sight? I want to go into one of the helping professions."

"I'd check it out, Renay. I'm sure it's a possibility."

A physical therapist who attended our church said the same thing. "There are great physical therapy schools at the College of St. Catherine, or St. Kate's, in Minneapolis, and the University of Wisconsin at both Superior and LaCrosse. Call the program directors and see if they can accommodate visually impaired students."

I learned that the telephone company had a free directory information program for visually impaired customers and I made good use of it as I contacted the schools. "It's about a two-year program to become a physical therapy assistant. And we've had successful visually impaired students. How much college coursework have you done?"

As Connie looked over the brochures that came in the mail, I said, "They're all so far away. I can't leave you and the girls for weeks at a time, and you don't have time to come and get me."

"Let's check into buses," she answered. We found out that I could use the Eau Claire Passenger Shuttle, a van that made daily trips to the Minneapolis airport. That would let me come home every weekend from St. Kate's. With Connie beside me each step of the way, I continued to explore attending St. Catherine's.

"I never even considered college," I said as Connie read the course descriptions to me. "How am I going to pass anatomy and physiology classes?"

"St. Catherine's learning center for the visually impaired is described here," Connie told me. "They have special equipment and skeletal models. You've always been able to learn anything you put your mind to."

"Thanks for the vote of confidence, but . . . I don't know. I don't know if I can do this. If I'm just going to fail, I should find something to do here in Eau Claire."

"Renay, the idea of physical therapy has stuck with you for weeks. I guess I don't know either, the classes will be so hard, but I think you should give it a try," Connie said as she gave my hand a squeeze. "It'll be tough on all of us, but you and I both know that you won't be satisfied flipping burgers. Two years and you'll have the kind of job you want once again."

We made the decision over a period of several months. When I asked the DVR counselor about schooling, she said, "You can't enroll anywhere. You're still on Cray's employee

98

list." She actually screamed at me and I wondered why a system that was supposed to help people find employment was trying to keep me unemployed.

I checked into occupational therapy, certain branches of nursing, and other health professions, but I kept returning to physical therapy. I'd be moving about, I had the physical strength to help nearly anyone, and I'd be working with people again.

I can do this. Maybe. I hope. God, I prayed, am I right? There's every reason to try?

A couple of sentences from St. Kate's program description echoed in my mind: "PTAs help people of all ages recover physical function and strength lost through diseases, injury, or other causes. They also help relieve pain and promote healing." I'd be helping people just like me. I knew how hard recovery could be. There was every reason to try.

The difference between living and making a living is a simple question, "How much must I pay you to settle for being unhappy?"

13

As Kara's third birthday approached, in spite of my pre-occupation with finding a new career, one nagging desire caught hold and wouldn't go away. I had always assumed I'd build a play structure for Alea and Kara—a palace, with swings and a slide and a platform "tree house" that would far outshine the one Randy, Gary, and I had built so many years before.

Building a Dream

CERTAIN THAT NO ONE was home to wonder at my clumsy actions, I paced off the backyard. From the garden to the fence—plenty of room for a swingset and the platform tower I envisioned. Somehow, Kara and Alea were going to have a swingset.

That night I told Connie my plans. "Can't we just buy one at Sears?" she asked.

"It wouldn't be the same," I sighed. "Think of what the girls could do with the tree house section. It'd be their fort, their palace, a sailing ship—Randy, Gary, and I spent *weeks* in the ramshackle one we built."

"I understand what you're thinking of, but how will we build it?"

I was an electrician, not a carpenter. "We need to go to Menard's. Someone there can help me work out the details."

Connie said, "What help will I be at Menard's? Could a friend take you?"

I knew just who to call: John and Karen Manydeeds. Kara and their daughter Jenay were already great buddies. Jenay would probably be on our swingset as much as our own girls. I called John, told him of my dream, and asked, "Would you go with me to the hardware store to price out the lumber and other supplies?"

"I'm an attorney, not a builder, Renay," he said.

"I think it's better that way—you won't let the store talk me into anything I can't handle."

Karen, whose bubbly laughter turned any outing into a treat, came along as well. The instant we walked into the store, we were greeted with, "Renay! So nice to see you." It was Wally, a basketball player I knew from the University of Eau Claire. He helped us select the right hammers, nails, and initial lumber needs.

John helped me stack the supplies in the garage and the lumber in the backyard. I still didn't know how I'd start. Restlessly, I debated with myself about whether it would be better to have two regular swings or a tire swing, a rope ladder or an extra slide, monkey bars or a climbing net. I hefted my old hammer and brainstormed how I would measure and cut accurately. Still unemployed, the dreams let me look forward to accomplishing something.

I knew I couldn't build it alone, but how could I ask anyone to show up for a month of Saturdays to build a wish, not a necessity? I needed so many favors from people for more important things like house projects that required borrowing someone's eyes. Yet, if I never built it, I'd somehow feel I'd failed as a father. It *had* to work out, somehow.

I told Connie, "I know it sounds impossible, but I so wish to have it done this summer that I'm just sure it will happen." When friends asked me about plans for the summer, I said I was building a swingset. "I'm just waiting for a spare pair of eyes," I joked.

Then a man came to our front door. "I was just passing through, visiting friends who live down the block a ways," he said, "and I'm out of work. I heard you might need a hand building a swingset?"

"A good pair of eyes wouldn't hurt, either," I said. "But I can't pay carpenter's wages."

He laughed. "All I need is a good hot meal or two and a few bucks. Mostly the meals. When do we start?"

Together we headed to the backyard where I knelt down and traced onto the grass a basic plan of the palace I had in mind for my girls. For a moment, I felt like I was running a crew at work again, explaining what needed to be done. The next moment, my thoughts turned to prayers of thankfulness, my face to one big smile, for help dressed as a stranger.

That first day, he looked over my plans and made some suggestions. We precut much of the lumber. He promised to return soon. "I'm so grateful for your offer," I said as we shook hands.

"The pleasure's mine. I'd rather help you out than sit idly this summer waiting for something to happen."

"Let me at least get your favorite meal ready for our first day of work. What is it?"

"Well, I love everything, and I doubt you'd be able to rustle up a skilletfull of sunfish fillets."

I laughed, "We just froze a day's catch. They'll be sizzling for you."

"I'm drooling already!"

While we didn't have a regular schedule, this stranger, whose name was John, showed up every Saturday, and several other days as well. He must have been in his mid-thirties, about the same age as me. We worked together in the summer heat, even in the rain, and he quickly learned to avoid my inaccuracies with a twelve-ounce hammer! Soon, the 8' x 8' platform rose solidly above my little domain.

Talk about a lesson in trusting a stranger! We had to learn to work in unison. I steadied lumber while he sawed and pounded close to my hands. I had to carefully listen to instructions, trying to understand and interpret his requests while my mind wandered and drifted with thoughts of the fun Kara and Alea would have when we finished.

Once the main structure was solid and secure, John cut the wood and laid out the hardware for the swings and slides. As his time with us grew short, he readied all the supplies for the ladder and the monkey bars, then showed Connie how to assemble them.

The girls, with sandpaper in hand, smoothed out each of the two-by-fours and dowels that would form the ladder. Then they took turns squeezing a bit of glue into the predrilled holes and pounding in the dowels (occasionally pounding my hands).

Kara, with a three-year-old's love of arts and crafts, filled the first hole entirely with glue. Connie exclaimed, "There's glue squirting out everywhere!"

It took a bit of sanding to clean up that first hole, but Kara caught on to the idea of "Just a little glue, honey."

After a few days' drying time, we carried the seven-foot ladders from the garage to "Poirier's Palace," with the girls holding one end, Connie in the middle, and me at the rear.

After Connie and I moved three yards of fine beach sand from the driveway via wheelbarrow, the four of us climbed aboard, with me feeling quite like a captain setting sail for a new shore. The awe in Alea and Kara's voices captivated my imagination, letting me know that "Poirier's Palace" would fill their heads with plenty of dreams and fulfill the promise I had made that my children would have a tree house like my boyhood haven.

The day before, we'd put the slide in place. Connie and I had lifted the girls up to the platform over and over. Now, with the ladders ready, Kara and Alea couldn't climb and slide fast enough to suit themselves. I stationed myself near the bottom of the slide and listened to the laughter, only occasionally receiving a loving smack on the head as little hands reached out for me.

As for the stranger, he disappeared before we completed those finishing touches, off, I'm sure, to help someone else. To this day, gazing at that play structure inspires me to help whomever, wherever, with whatever they need. You don't need to see to lend a strong back for shoveling concrete while pouring someone's driveway or to hold Sheetrock overhead. Who knows, you might be just the angel someone needs, outfitted with a hammer instead of a halo to make a dream come true, as did mine.

God is no stranger, for he is always in our hearts,
ready to appear to others through our actions
when we use the gifts he gave us.

14

While I hammered and sanded the wood for the jungle gym, I agonized over the decision to enroll in St. Kate's Physical Therapy Assistant program. Could I commute from Eau Claire to Minneapolis for two and a half years?

What about my family? The extra burdens on Connie? With all of the time we'd had together, how could I stand being away from Alea and Kara? Wasn't there another career that would allow me to stay in Eau Claire?

The answer kept coming back, You can do this. You'll be able to help people again. It will work. Perhaps my mother's example helped me step out in faith.

Together While Apart

WHEN I WAS in fifth grade, Mom gathered all of us together in our little living room and said, "This summer we're starting a new adventure together. Shanon," she said, giving my youngest sister a little hug, "will be a great big first grader this fall. All of us will be in school, including me! I've been accepted into nursing school."

Even as a ten-year-old, I could see the hints of hope and pride in her face as she continued. "Adventures are never easy, but we need to better ourselves as a family. After I become a nurse, we might even be able to have a car! But here's the tough part. . . ."

Mom took a deep breath before she continued. "I'll be studying every night . . . and we'll only have a tiny apartment, smaller than this. So, Randy and Renay and Kim will come with me and go to school for a year in Superior. Shanon, Rhonda—you get to spend the year with Grandma and Grandpa Meier! They're getting my old room all ready for you!"

The room was silent for a moment. I watched Rhonda's eyes grow wide, Shanon's chin start to tremble. Inside, I could feel my stomach flip-flop as I tried to comprehend what she was saying. Leave two sisters behind? Rhonda, who was eight, spoke first. "But Mom. . . ."

"This will be the hardest year ever, but we need to pull together as a family. Remember, your brothers and Kim will have to start all over in a strange school. Let's figure out how we're going to help each other through this."

We had about three months to ready ourselves for the move, which we made in July. Mom made it clear that we couldn't take many things with us. Randy and I managed to fit almost all our earthly possessions in one box: our Matchbox cars, plastic army men, marbles, and the baseball gloves Grandpa Meier had given each of us. Kim brought a few dolls and her jump rope. The bike we shared stayed in Bloomer.

Grandpa rented a truck to haul our few belongings to Superior, where Mom had found a small apartment. Randy and I helped load up a couple of beds, a box of pots and pans, and our clothes and toys.

Our new home took up half of an old, two-story brick house. The neighborhood was a mix of turn-of-the-century homes converted into apartments and newer bungalows that had replaced older homes. Dirt alleys and cracked sidewalks, elms and oaks that towered higher than the rooftops, and narrow walkways between the buildings all added to the antiquated feel of the street.

To get to our front door, we climbed the steps to the porch we shared with the people in the other apartment. The view out our bedroom window was of the building next door, no more than four feet away.

It didn't take us long to unload everything, even with having to haul everything up the steps. The apartment had wooden floors and arches over doors. All the trim was decoratively painted in harvest gold and brown. The front door opened onto our living room, a ten-foot-square room with high ceilings. Mom and Grandpa placed an old upholstered chair there. Springs showed through a hole in the cushion and the arms were already worn from being sat on—three children to one chair. A matching couch—matching in protruding stuffing and springs, not color—and a folding chair completed our furniture collection. A short corridor behind the living room led to the narrow kitchen. There was just enough room for the four-foot table we'd brought, but we soon found out that when all four of us sat down for a meal, it was crowded. No going to the bathroom once food was on the table!

Mom tucked her bedroom and study area under the stairs off the kitchen. For a desk, she topped some wooden crates with beat-up boards we found in the alley by the garbage cans. When she had to write papers, she placed a cutting board from the kitchen over the boards; they were too rough to write legibly on. But by studying there instead of in the living room, she left the downstairs free for the three of us to play. Kim often colored while we played with cars, but we also played hide-and-seek and other games that she joined in on.

The stairs led up to the bathroom and the one bedroom, where Randy and I shared a single bed. The room was so small that we could barely close the door. Kim's room was a former coat closet down the hall.

The bathroom had an old rusty tub and fixtures. The walls were painted a nice shade of green, but much of it was peeling away. Randy and I still remembered using the farm's outhouse before we moved to Bloomer, so any indoor plumbing was fine with us.

With our few worldly goods, Randy and I felt like early pioneers. Not having a car meant that even finding a grocery store was an adventure. Lake Superior was a half mile away—not a beach, but a walkway where we could watch the waves and the sea gulls.

The old wringer washing machine stayed in Bloomer. Mom found a rickety wagon at a thrift sale to use for trips to the laundromat. Randy and I carried it, loaded with clothes, to the sidewalk. Mom always brought down another armload of jeans or shirts to pile on top. Kim stretched out on top of the clothes to keep them from falling off or blowing away. Mom pulled the wagon, squeaking and rattling, while Randy and I walked alongside, making sure that neither Kim nor our clothes fell out as we made our way to the Laundromat.

Often we brought our toy cars along, making garages for them out of empty detergent boxes. We raced them down the rows of machines, checking for spare change under the dryers as we went. Rather than spend our precious nickels on dryers, we'd carefully place all of the wet clothes back in the wagon, head home, and hang them out to dry on the lines back by the alley.

Randy, Kim, and I had a few weeks to explore Superior before school opened in September. A park not far from our apartment boasted swings, an open field for playing catch, and a swimming hole, kind of a backwater off of Lake

Superior. We spent hours splashing around and looking for agates. Mom started classes almost immediately, but she took the time to take us down to Lake Superior. The water is icy even on the hottest of summer days. We'd walk along the sandy shore, every so often kicking our feet at the lapping waves. Often, Mom grew quiet. I knew she was thinking how much Rhonda and Shanon would enjoy the lake, too.

Our school was about half a mile from the apartment, but Mom had to walk much farther. On rainy days, she wrapped her books in Bunny Bread wrappers with rubber bands, then tucked them inside her coat to keep them dry. Usually we arrived home long before she did. It was Randy's and my job to help Kim, a second grader, with any homework she had. Mom's rules for school were simple: Respect your teachers, do the best you can, and ask for help when you need it. She told us, "Make sure you ask questions at school. I won't have time to spend going through your homework."

Mom got to know some of the other women in nursing school. Two older students took her under their wings and gave her rides, so that some of the time she was there when we got home from school.

One day as we rounded the corner onto our street, a cry greeted us. Mom was out on our porch, decked out in a triangular cardboard hat and a paper eye patch. Ribbons blocked us from climbing the front steps. "Nay, lads and lassie, ye'll not be boarding this ship 'til ye be bringin' me treasure. Now off with ye!"

Our faces must have looked blank, for she added, "Rare stones, lost pennies, precious flowers—off with ye, see what ye be findin'!" We dumped our schoolbooks on the steps and raced off on the first of many treasure hunts.

The pirate game surfaced throughout the year. I remember complaining about a math problem one night, only to hear Mom mutter in reply, "Aye, ye'll walk the plank,

young laddie, if you don't be larnin' the dividin' and multi-
plyin.' "

If Mom headed back to school to study at night, we had
to stay inside. Then we'd break off tree branches and have
sword fights or practice dribbling a basketball in the "gym,"
our all-purpose living room. One winter day, Randy and I
went searching for treasure right in our apartment, probing
under the baseboards for scraps of paper or tiny pebbles that
had rolled there. I discovered an 1898 Indian head penny;
that tells you how old the house was! We fished for it with a
coat hanger for two afternoons before we finally dug it out.

Pretending we were pirates, making laundry day into a
fun outing despite the squeaky wagon, enjoying the lake—
looking back, I can see how hard Mom worked to help us
all make the best of our year in exile. Mom said, "It's our
desert wandering, just like the Israelites had to wander in the
desert before reaching the Promised Land."

I think we three children adjusted fairly quickly. The
school was bigger than we were used to, but all three of us
found new friends. We had to. Mom made it clear that we
wouldn't be visiting Bloomer until Christmastime.

I thought that we couldn't go home because of all the
homework Mom had. But late one night, maybe a month
after we settled in, I saw the light on in Mom's room. I could
hear her sniffling. At first I wondered if she was coming
down with a cold, but as I peeked around her doorway,
I saw the tears that filled her sad eyes with the pain of
loneliness.

I said, "Mom, would a hug help?"

She wiped the back of her hand across her eyes, then
hugged me tight. "Renay, I just want us all to be together."

The mournful note of a train whistle sounded from the
nearby tracks as I sat by Mom's side. She sighed and said,
"We're going to be like that little train that said 'I think I can,

I think I can. . . .' We just need to be strong together and stay focused. We'll make it just fine."

I nodded, wondering how I could be strong for her. It also dawned on me that we couldn't *afford* to go home. Mom didn't have bus fare for all of us. In truth, we barely had shoes. Randy and I tried out for the Superior Hoop Club basketball team, despite my black high-top tennis shoes that displayed my socks to the world through the top, bottom and heel. The coach said, "Tell your mom to get you some new shoes," but we didn't have the money. I played all year in those sneakers, flopping up and down the court.

That night, after seeing Mom cry, I prayed until I fell asleep, staring out our tiny window at the stars. *God, help Mom get her wish so she won't be sad.* I knew then how alone she felt, away from her friends, her parents, and two of her precious daughters.

Perhaps that's why God sent so many people to help us. Looking back, I saw the face of God so many times through that year.

First, there was the couple who owned the television repair shop. We'd brought our old thirteen-inch black and white TV to Superior, but some of the vacuum tubes must have cracked during the bumpy truck ride from Bloomer. In November, as the shorter daylight hours kept us inside more, Mom tucked the TV into the wagon and pulled it over to a repair shop. She told the owner, "We can't afford much . . . if you can do anything at all."

The gentleman looked at our TV, then went into the back room and called to his wife before saying, "We have a spare TV that you can use, say, for a dollar a week." That meant we could watch *I Love Lucy* and *Mr. Magoo* again.

Mom tried to return the TV when we went back to Bloomer, but he wouldn't hear of it. "No, you've paid for it by now."

Mom told us, "Maybe a TV isn't very important, considering all the things we need, but I can't look at it without thinking, 'The Lord's watching over us.' Think how blessed we were to get it, all through the kindness of strangers. Knowing that God was looking out for us helped me study and continue on the path toward nursing. Now we need to find some way to help the Lord."

Then there was Grenache's Candy Store. After school in Superior, we passed Mr. Grenache's big bay window where you could stand and watch him swirl apples through a creamy golden pan of caramel. He was an old fellow, with a nice big smile full of wrinkles. He still had a thick crop of white hair, just like St. Nick. His wife was a bit more stout, giving her a merry round face, rosy cheeks, and white hair to match her husband's. Occasionally, we stepped inside just to savor the wonderful aromas; we couldn't afford candy. But one day, as we stuck our noses in, the old man reached into his jar of homemade caramels and tossed three of them our way. A thin, crystallized coating around the outside, soft and creamy inside—I can still taste it. "Thank you," we chimed.

After that it was hard to stay away. The Grenaches soon became our grandparents away from home, listening to our stories of school, home, and friendships.

That God was truly taking care of us became a fact for me at Christmas. Finally, we were headed back to Bloomer to see our sisters. Grandpa mailed Mom a check that covered the bus fare home for all four of us. The evenings before Christmas were spent helping Mother stuff the rag dolls she'd made for Shanon and Rhonda, getting all of our schoolwork done, buying fruit and water for the bus ride. At last, the day arrived to pack our clothes, our favorite Lake Superior rocks, the pictures we'd drawn for our grandparents, and a treat of Grenache's caramels into the pillowcases we used for suitcases.

With our pillowcases in hand, we must have looked like transients searching for a place to sleep as we walked to the bus depot. Mom walked to the ticket window with Grandpa's check. The man glanced at it and said, "We can't accept out of town checks, and certainly not third-person ones." He handed it back.

Mom stammered, "Is, is there anything I can do to change your mind?"

"No, the policy doesn't allow it."

Behind us was a woman in a brown coat with a black collar and huge buttons. She overheard, and said, "I'll take that check for you." Before Mom could say a word, she opened her purse and counted out the bills.

"Merry Christmas," she said as she pressed the money in to Mom's hand. Both women were smiling in excitement. A glowing warmth seemed to fill the air around them.

"Thank you. God bless. . . ." Mom managed to say through her tears. We'd witnessed the blessings of giving and receiving.

A pebble drops in a lake. First the splash,
then the magical formation of uniform circles,
waves radiating outward in search of
their resting places. So too must we
share the word and
love of God.

15

Connie wholeheartedly supported my decision to enter St. Catherine's, even as we agonized over how we could afford the tuition. As I searched for sources, my gratitude grew for the two monumental things that happened when I was fourteen. I met my wife and I found my car.

The Car

THE GYM of my school was packed with squirming junior high students assembled together for a concert given by St. Paul's, the Catholic school in Bloomer.

To me, any kind of assembly was a welcome break from classes. As the band broke into a Sousa march, I wondered whether my sisters would like or hate the school uniforms the girls wore—blue and black plaid jumpers with white blouses.

Then, in that sea of sameness, something about a certain saxophone player caught my eye. Her long, reddish brown hair? The freckles? The twinkling smile she sent my way?

As soon as the concert was over, I ran over to hold the door open for her, figuring she could use help maneuvering that sax through the swinging doors. I said "Hi" and she answered back. That was all.

I didn't even know her name until ninth grade, when we both enrolled at Bloomer High School. Even without the plaid uniform, I immediately recognized her in the hallway. This time I managed to ask, "So, what's your name?" and carry her books.

A movie was our first date. I walked over to Connie's, met her parents, and then walked her to the theater on Bloomer's main street. I couldn't drive yet and riding bikes to a movie with a date didn't seem very romantic.

Even if I'd been old enough to drive, though, I wouldn't have wanted to take my mom's ancient car, a junker of a Rambler complete with a huge fantail rear. Before Mom finished school, we'd had nothing but bikes and the rickety wagon. I knew that Rambler was all we could afford, and I was mature enough to appreciate having any car, such as it was. However, I dreamed of saving enough for new wheels before I had my license for very long.

Walking Connie home from school, carrying her books, was soon part of my routine, so much so that I got to know her neighbors and the cars they drove. One day, a radiant new maroon car purred past us before pulling into the driveway next door.

It was love at first sight, just like spotting Connie in the band. I stared after the car for such a long time that Connie finally said, "That must be our neighbor Marilyn's dad, Jerry. He owns the garage in town, you know." She waved as the man climbed out of the car, then took me over to meet him.

After shaking his hand, I said, "That sure is a swell car."

Jerry smiled. "It's a Pontiac Catalina. Just once, I wanted a V-8 engine, the kind that propels a car down the highway with no more than a tap on the gas pedal." As he spoke, I peered in through the window, catching a glimpse of plush cloth upholstery and a backseat wide enough to hold all the children in my family.

Jerry said, "Hop in the back, you two. We'll head around the block."

What a treat, sitting in the backseat of the car of my dreams with Connie. The car's engine hummed like a well-tuned orchestra as Jerry showed us what it could do.

After that afternoon, I must admit my attention was divided between Connie and the car. If Jerry drove up while the two of us were playing football, the car usually won out.

Jerry was the same age as my grandparents, and his only daughter was all grown up. Perhaps he enjoyed passing on his love of cars—or perhaps he just took pity on a boy without a father. Whatever his reasons, I was welcome at his garage any time.

There was nothing fancy about Jerry's service garage, just a one-stall concrete building, but Jerry didn't need anything fancy to keep every car in town running as smoothly as his Catalina. He was at least six feet tall, although a bit hunched from all those years spent bending over car engines. His hands were rough and nicked from tackling rusty wheel nuts, but the lines on his face all came from smiling.

Sometimes Jerry let me help him wash the Catalina. That car was babied as if it were a Rolls Royce. If Jerry saw me walking through town, he'd give me a lift to his service garage, which was right next to the middle school playground. There, I'd help systematically remove any speck of dirt, dust, or insect, inside and out. "Our cars, and our lives, run better when we keep them clean," he told me.

Other afternoons, Jerry let me "help" change the oil. I handed him rags, opened cans, and crawled under the car with him so he could show me exactly how to keep a car in perfect shape.

I found I could talk about anything with Jerry. One afternoon, after I'd complained about algebra, he put down his wrench, wiped his hands on a rag, and pulled out a pad of paper. "Algebra's important if you ever want to work on cars. Here, this is how you figure out how much oil you need," he said as his pencil sped across the paper. He added a couple of problems on timing a car for me to work out.

Some days, with a twinkle in his eye, he'd ask, "How's that girl?" He knew I still saw Connie almost every day, for he often picked us up if he saw us walking together.

Best of all, though, were the days he'd say, "Let's take her out for a spin." I know it only happened a few times over the summer, and we only drove fifteen or twenty miles. Yet part of me feels like I spent a lifetime in the passenger seat of that car, talking with Jerry. Actually, we shouted back and forth since both of us loved having all the windows rolled down.

The first time we headed out together, Jerry popped open the glove compartment and pointed to the St. Christopher medal taped inside. "That's not for good luck," he told me, "but a reminder that driving is dangerous. A bit of prayer mixed in with common sense goes a long way."

But my junior year, my family moved to Chippewa Falls. I don't know which hurt more, losing touch with Connie or with Jerry. Connie and I parted cordially, at least on the surface, saying that we'd be too far apart to have a meaningful relationship, but inside, I wondered if anyone in the world could be as much fun to be with as Connie.

Saying I'd never love again seemed a bit dramatic, but I finished high school without finding anyone so special. During my senior year, back in Bloomer, Connie and I talked and told each other we were still friends, but we both dated other people.

Some things, though, are just meant to be. After I graduated, I moved to Eau Claire, a bigger town where I could work toward becoming an electrician. Again, I dated, but couldn't seem to meet anyone that made days together seem only minutes long.

Almost four years passed. One Saturday, friends talked me into going to Shenanigan's, a local restaurant with a dance floor. And, out on that dance floor, was Connie. With the feeling that this couldn't be happening, that I had to be dreaming, that this was the stuff of movies, I glided up behind her, tapped her shoulder, and murmured, "Would you like to dance, good-looking?"

I think both of us were trying to act nonchalant; we almost forgot to exchange phone numbers. She was finishing her teaching degree at the university in town. "Call me when you aren't too busy studying," I said as I gave her a quick peck on the cheek.

Months went by. I'd been so sure she'd call. I began to tell myself that it was crazy to think she'd be interested in someone from high school. I had almost adjusted to a life without Connie when my phone rang. A collect call from Florida. "I . . . well . . ." her sweet voice said, "no one here dances like you."

We talked for three hours. I had to work overtime to pay off the phone bill. But I knew I was going to marry her.

In 1984, the year Connie and I married, the '74 Pontiac Catalina came back into my life as well.

Jerry's daughter called, tracking me down through Connie's folks. She let me know that Jerry had passed away.

"I . . . I'm so sorry," I said, stunned.

She said, "We had lots of time to say good-bye to each other. Dad kept talking these past few months about all the fun you two had with that big old car. He said, 'Give the kid first chance to buy it if he wants it.' "

Only 20,000 miles on it, only two thousand dollars for it. We sold my '65 Ford Fairlane that very day, and I owned the car of my dreams.

Now I was behind the wheel, not Jerry. I tried to imagine myself, the boy of ten years before. What had Jerry seen as

I sat beside him on the passenger side? A lonely teenager? A budding mechanic? Simply a boy who loved this car as much as he did?

I babied that car just like Jerry had. Each week I checked the oil and fluids, tested the belts, crawled under the chassis to look for leaks, vacuumed the interior with its still-immaculate upholstery, and polished the windows inside and out. Every time I drove it or worked on it, I felt like I was having a chat with Jerry.

By 1990, the mileage was up to around 100,000, but I'd kept the rust at bay. The battery and muffler needed replacing, but I knew how. It needed new tires, too. I knew just which ones I wanted, a bit sportier than standard issue, worthy of my car.

The last time I drove it was the day I lost my sight. That Pontiac wasn't just a car to me, but an anchor, a connection with the man who had stepped in for the father I didn't have. The day a friend drove it to my mom's, parking it in a field alongside the garage, another piece of me died. Not driving was bad enough, but here I had to say good-bye to Jerry all over.

At first I couldn't sell it. In fact, once or twice I crawled into the front seat just to feel the steering wheel in my hands one more time. I listened to the engine, imagining once again the feel of the tools in my hand I'd used to fix it so often.

By the time I'd decided to complete physical therapy training at St. Kate's, I knew I needed the car for a different purpose. By selling it, I could get part of the money I needed for tuition.

When a woman with three children in tow came to see it, I knew Jerry would approve. That car needed a purpose, a good home. I sat in the front seat one last time, flipped open the glove compartment, and removed Jerry's St.

Christopher medal. Later, I tucked the image of the saint of wayfarers into my wallet, where it could travel with me on this new adventure in my life.

The car and Connie—they'd always been tangled together in the web of things I loved. Saying good-bye to the car, though, heightened for me how lucky I was to have the kind of wife I had, who stuck by me for better or for worse. I knew I could live without the car, but that night I said a silent prayer of thanks to a God who helped me reunite with a very special saxophone player.

If we pass up the joy of living today,
we're passing up all we've got
for something we hope to get.

16

As the start of classes at St. Kate's drew near, I struggled with being away from my girls so much. How could I protect them? Wasn't that a parent's role?

Fear Not!

THE SKIES ABOVE Bloomer turned an ominous shade of green one summer afternoon when I was about seven years old. Randy and I came in from playing baseball as soon as the first huge drops of rain hit the sidewalk, because the wind and the air had an eerie feel. Before we could climb the stairs to our apartment, the town tornado siren sounded.

Mom came out the door, our sisters in tow, calling our names. Relieved to see us on the steps, she hollered, "Get to the storm cellar. Now!" Randy and I scampered to hold the front door open for Mom. By this time, the wind was howling so fiercely that we could barely hear each other yell. All of us ran toward the steps, but the winds picked up little Shanon and tossed her off the porch. Randy and I caught up with her twenty feet away and dragged her toward the cellar doors, where Mom was already pulling on the handles that covered what was actually the root cellar, the house's only shelter for storms.

That cellar was one place that not even Randy and I played. Damp, dark, full of spiderwebs, it hardly seemed safe on the nicest of days. However, with the wind lashing around us, we gladly leaped down those steps.

Mom slammed the doors after us, then sat down on the bottom step so that we could gather around her. Between the wind and the thunder, nature seemed to be crashing and scratching against the cellar doors, like a giant animal trying to claw its way in after us. Mom started singing a song as she wrapped her arms more tightly around all five of us.

As the lightning flashed, I could see the fear in my siblings' faces. Mom laughed as she looked at us, saying, "It's just the angels taking pictures. They're having a great time, bowling. Oh there, someone got a strike," she said after a particularly loud crack of thunder. Gradually, we all relaxed in her care. The storm passed quickly with little damage to the town other than broken tree branches and the removal of a few loose shingles here and there.

The image of my mother, sheltering all of us in the darkness, stayed with me. It symbolized the kind of parent I wanted to be: a shelter of safety and refuge for my children. But how do you guard your children from dangers when you can't even see where they are?

For the first few months of darkness, I feared accidentally hurting Kara or Alea. What if I stepped on our crawling infant or tripped into Alea, as I had our poor cat Punkin? I sometimes crawled around the house myself, feeling foolish yet confident that I was avoiding disaster. Or, more simply, what if I missed a brewing case of diaper rash? Connie probably despaired at the amount of ointment I used to avoid this predicament.

Our house was well childproofed, though. I did my best to relax and find ways to have fun with our girls. Some things didn't change. Alea had learned months before how ticklish my feet were. Now that I couldn't see, her game of sneaking up on me while my feet occupied the living room footstool took on new excitement. Often, I heard her giggles long before I felt her fingers, but then my game became keeping the smile off my face and letting her "surprise" me. I didn't dare move my feet for fear of kicking her—what a target I was, a sitting duck!

Punkin helped me out, too. Alea would plunk him on my lap, then fetch the cat's brush. Together we groomed him and talked about how you take care of those you love. "That's why we help you take baths and dry your hair and brush your teeth," I told her.

Punkin was probably the best-groomed cat in town since it was something in which I could fully participate. I wondered, though, if we were overdoing it when Connie asked me, "Did you tell Alea to brush Punkin's teeth? She had the cat between her knees, with toothpaste smeared all over his whiskers!"

Gradually, we found other activities, like building forts with foam blocks; it didn't matter who or what they fell onto when the walls tumbled. We made bread together in the bread machine; Alea learned early on how to help me measure and pour for the recipes I knew by heart. We played games, too, like Monopoly, Life, and Sorry; Alea, then Kara, mastered keeping track of my playing pieces and theirs.

But we couldn't stay inside all the time. I knew that, yet to venture out, unable to easily keep track of the girls, sent my stomach churning. How could I keep them safe if I couldn't see where they were?

Any control I had over those fears dissipated one afternoon when Alea and I were out for a stroll. I thought we were safely by the side of the road. Suddenly, tires squealed in front of us. My heart pounding, I pulled my crying daughter into my arms, not knowing which way to turn. The motorist yelled out, "Keep your kid out of the road, you weirdo."

It was weeks before I dared to leave our yard again without Connie, but the yard wasn't completely safe, either. One afternoon the girls were playing on our jungle gym while I putzed with something by the back door. Suddenly, Alea screamed, "Bear! Daddy, Daddy, Bear!"

I thought they were playing a game but then sensed the lack of fun in their voices. I walked toward the jungle gym and heard them come down the slide. The cat brushed against my leg as the girls ran by. They must have had Punkin on a leash. When the cat hit me, I turned around, then spotted a huge black shape next to me. Now I screamed, "Bear" and ran toward the house. Even with my arms outstretched, I ran smack into the big ash tree on the way and had to scramble up the steps on all fours.

Connie was in the front yard, and I yelled to her to get inside. She said, "There it is, between our house and the neighbors. That explains why the police are down at the end of the block!"

There hasn't been a bear in our neighborhood since. I think we scared him as much as he scared us. It wasn't bears in particular that scared me, but rather the incident was like a giant exclamation mark that summed up my inability to protect my daughters.

At the mall one day, Connie left me with the girls for just a minute to look at something. Within twenty seconds, Alea tripped and fell, resulting in twenty stitches in her forehead.

As Alea began riding a bike, I stayed right next to her for days to make sure she had her balance. But the first time I let her venture off toward the playground ahead of me, I heard a clatter and a scream. "Alea," I called, trying to determine just where she was.

"Daddy," her howls continued, growing closer. I wanted to run, but instead had to slow down for fear of tripping over the bike and landing on her. At last, I was by her side and she whimpered, "My knee, it's bleeding."

Cautiously, I felt along her leg, detecting the roughness of scrapes and pebbles ground into her skin. She grabbed me around the neck as I lifted her up. I started to take a step, then realized that I didn't know which way home was. In hurrying toward Alea, I'd lost all sense of direction. "Alea, which way is home?" I whispered, holding her tight. Guilt washed through me as my little girl heroically directed me home, even through her pain and fright.

I even failed on family trips to the beach. Connie left us safely on the sand while she made a quick trip to the beach house, and I managed to cut my own foot on a piece of glass. At least it wasn't one of the girls.

COUNTLESS TIMES I relived the Sunday before the accident, jumping over and over into a pile of leaves Alea and I had raked together. How I longed to do that with Kara, or to take both girls by the hand and run through the park without a care.

Instead, I kept the girls close by my side, and even checked into buying electronic monitoring devices so they couldn't wander from the yard without my knowing. I kept wondering, *God, it's so obvious that I can't protect my daughters. Can't you send a couple of your best guardian angels our way? Please?* On the one hand, events kept proving that there were very real things to fear. On the other hand, I knew I was in danger of making the girls overly fearful. I needed to deal with my own fears head-on if I was going to be any kind of father to them.

I started recalling other images from my childhood. The time Randy tried to toboggan under a barbed-wire fence and ended up with a row of stitches. The time the toboggan flipped on top of me—my turn for stitches. Yet we wouldn't have given up sledding for anything. We had way too much fun with it.

As much a source of shelter as our mother was, she hadn't kept me from every harm. And, how awful it would have been if she'd always kept us in sight as she cared for our little sisters! Randy and I somehow lived through climbing trees and wading in the creek and jumping from the roof of the beach house. The fun we had, not knowing we were risking our necks! I had to find ways to let go of my girls while still caring for them.

Forcefully setting my fears aside opened up all kinds of creativity that I used to find solutions. First, I made a game out of describing where we were. "There's a beautiful willow tree here at the park, isn't there? We could almost play hide-and-seek in the long branches that sweep around it. But Alea, can you look by the swings carefully? Is there any broken glass? Kara? Tell me about who else is at the park today."

I listened for bird calls I recognized, then said, "Look in the branches above, isn't there a bright red bird? That whistle belonged to a cardinal. Can you see one?"

Parent-child swimming lessons helped me gain confidence in my daughters' abilities. At first, Alea's aim in jumping to me wasn't very good; sometimes she landed in front of me, sometimes right on top of me. Yet every time I finally got hold of her, she giggled and spit water onto my face. Gradually I relaxed and enjoyed blowing bubbles and letting her follow the instructor's directions. Eventually, Connie just dropped the two of us off at the pool and Alea guided me through the locker rooms. It was our time together.

Connie and I sought out other controlled situations where I could drop my guard. For example, Alea and Kara learned to in-line skate on a nearby tennis court: smooth surface, fences to hold on to, boundaries on where they could go.

Always, we looked for ways to create borders so the girls knew what we expected and I could relax, at least a little! At Fourth of July fireworks, we spread out a sleeping bag and asked the girls to stay on it, or in it if the night air grew chilly. At the University of Eau Claire Blugold basketball games, Kara and Alea sat on the bleacher right in front of us. I casually placed a foot by their side so I knew where they were.

We learned other tricks as well, all to let me know that Alea and Kara were safe. For car trips, Connie taught the girls to keep their hands in their laps and their feet still until the doors were closed. I didn't want to slam a door only to hear a scream of pain. Or, they'd clap their hands so I knew they were out of the way.

Slowly, I learned to laugh at myself. At the county fair, we tried every roller coaster, every whirling and spinning ride, all together in the same cars. We jumped into piles of leaves again, too. I just had to go first so I wouldn't land on top of my girls!

Perhaps fishing helped me put things into perspective. For children, nothing beats going after sunfish on a sunny day. They come into shallow water warmed by the sun's rays; you can plop your line, complete with bobber, right under the nose of the fish you want to catch as they dart back and forth in the clear water.

However, fishing close to shore also means there are plenty of things to snag on—trees, weeds, even me occasionally. In the few times we went, we lost more bobbers, hooks and line than I had in all the rest of my life. I think I ended up with ten hooks *in* my hand as well (it took awhile to get the girls to understand that they had to hold the poles perfectly still while Daddy helped the fish off the hook!). But with the four of us close together in our just-the-right-size boat, and life jackets on the girls to keep my worries at bay, I learned to relax and enjoy our time together.

Once Alea hooked what seemed to her to be a monster fish. "Daddy, take the pole!" she yelled.

"No, you hold on tight," I said, sure she was exaggerating. "It's probably not a big one and its daddy would be mad if you didn't get it in here."

I heard Alea plop down on the boat seat. From the commotion, I could tell she was pulling with all her might. Connie exclaimed, "It's a bass, not a sunny!"

Getting that one off the line as it flipped and flopped took quite awhile. A three-pound bass can be pretty exciting.

The more we did together, the more I focused on fun. One afternoon we traveled to the woods where I'd often gone hunting. With the soft breeze on our faces, the leaves crunching beneath our feet, I had no trouble imagining the kind of perfect fall day we were enjoying. Quietly, we walked down a path, hoping to see some of the abundant wildlife.

In whispers, the girls told me, "Dad, there's a squirrel . . . another one . . . wow, a porcupine." Then, they stopped suddenly.

Connie murmured, "There's a deer, no two, a doe and a fawn, just off the path. They're heading toward us." Silently, we waited, standing perfectly still as the deer walked within ten feet of us before slowly moving away.

Alea said, "I didn't know their noses were black."

"And they've got whiskers!" Kara added.

That same day, a couple of squirrels came right up to the girls as well. It was almost magical, as if God had the animals put on a show for us. Through my daughters' vivid descriptions, I enjoyed our afternoon together as much as if I'd had my sight.

Like all parents, I still had fears for Alea and Kara's safety, but perhaps I learned a bit sooner than some that by ourselves we can't keep our children totally safe. I can pray for them, Connie and I can teach them our values, we can talk with them and watch over them. At some point, though, we have to hug them tight, then let go and say, "Lord, they're your children, too. Help us help them. Amen."

*Our happiness or unhappiness depends far more
on the way we meet the events of life
than on the nature of the
events themselves.*

17

A journey of a thousand miles begins with a single step. Even the longest journeys can seem more enjoyable with the right companions. While no one could fill the gap created by being away from home, my years at St. Catherine's were blessed with gifts from God—caring instructors and class-mates I'll never forget.

School Dazed

THERE I WAS, a thirty-five-year-old father of two, unpacking a box of supplies for my dorm room at St. Kate's. My talking clock, decorated with stickers by Alea and Kara—I didn't want to be late for class. A few changes of clothing—I'd do my laundry at home on the weekends. A couple of tape players for studying and for music to chase away loneliness. A little sculpted angel for the wall where I planned to keep the audiotape currently requiring study. There wasn't much else. I couldn't stare at pictures of my three girls. I certainly didn't care whether my room's curtains and bedspread matched.

I could hear Connie, Alea, and Kara opening dresser drawers, peeking in the little closet. "I'll just make sure you're organized," my wife said, "and then we'll head home. I don't want the girls going to bed late."

My stomach flip-flopped. They'd be two hours away from me at bedtime. I wouldn't be telling them stories tonight or tucking them in. Well, this was certainly no time to start rethinking my decision. I put a smile on my face and said, "Set all of my school supplies on the top bunk and I'll be fine. Let's explore the campus together for awhile." I didn't want to be alone in the room, not just yet.

We walked among the buildings for a half-hour or so, with Alea and Kara explaining to me what they saw. They jumped on and off the low-lying concrete walls that dotted the campus grounds. There was a playground area not too far from the school, and little Kara said, "Dad, you can go swinging there!"

Alea added, "There are so many trees, lots of shade so your head won't get sunburned."

We found spots between the buildings where our voices echoed; since I couldn't see, I didn't know whether anyone stared at us while we hooted and hollered. Then, all too quickly, Connie's arms were around my neck as she said good-bye.

"I'll be back Friday night," I reminded her, feeling much less self-assured than I hoped I sounded. The bloom was fading fast from the rose of my relief at finally starting school; tonight I'd be alone.

"Do you want us to show you where your room is again, Daddy?" Alea asked, always my shepherd.

"I'd better get used to finding it on my own, honey, but thanks," I said. I placed my hands on either side of her face and kissed her forehead. Hugs for everyone, and then they were gone.

A FEW VIVID memories stand out from those early days. Deb Churchill, my learning advisor, spent several hours helping me memorize building layouts, my class schedule, and making the arrangements for me to get recordings of the course textbooks. I had so much to learn before I could even start learning!

One of those first mornings, Deb read aloud to me from the student handbook. "Graduates of our program will be able to successfully demonstrate nine specific competencies; they will be able to administer the following techniques . . . gait training . . . independent living skills . . . orthotic and prosthetic devices . . . wound care . . . respond to acute changes in patients' physiologic state . . . perform standard measuring techniques. . . ."

Hearing that list brought alive for me what a physical therapist assistant actually *did*, not just the classes I had to take or the few treatments I'd experienced myself. In the space of a few paragraphs, my focus changed from whether I'd be able to pass my classes to whether I'd be able to learn enough to help my future patients.

During my first actual class, "Gross Anatomy and Kinesiology of the Musculoskeletal System," the instructor asked us to introduce ourselves. When my turn came, I stood up and said, "I'm Renay Poirier, I'm visually impaired, and I'd like to start a study group." The room stayed absolutely quiet (other than the pounding of my heart) as the instructor passed around slips of paper with my name and number on it. After class, people seemed to melt away. No one approached me about studying together, nor did anyone call me.

When a few days passed without a call, I reassured myself that no one had known me long enough to dislike me. Everyone was new to the program, uncertain of themselves; that's why they hadn't called. If I had to study on my own, I at least had the people from the learning center to help me.

For someone like me who had never given a thought to college before, two daunting tasks loomed before me: studying the textbooks I could only hear and memorizing the body's 206 bones and hundreds of muscles through the models I could only touch.

The first set of book tapes I received had four chapters recorded, then a quiz. I pushed the play button as soon as my alarm clock sounded in the morning. Often, I had to rewind to find the spot where I'd fallen asleep the night before. I still occasionally had nightmares about my accident; now these were joined by visions of threatening muscles surrounding me or doctors looming over me with accusations of incompetency.

I studied even harder. I labeled all the cassettes with a tape labeler, then used a toothpick to trace the letters and find the right tapes. The audio indexing feature of the recorder let me insert beeps at the start of each chapter; the recorder could then be fast-forwarded to those markers. However, that system didn't help me remember where the information was that I most needed to study in any given chapter. Eventually, I asked that the recordings be no more than an hour long, with the relevant questions asked at the end of each section. That helped immensely.

The lab work was a different magnitude of challenge— how do you feel the difference between the different arm or neck muscles? My first day in the lab, Deb Churchill spent over two hours helping me line up the materials I needed, sort the various audiotapes, and memorize the shape and feel of my first set of muscles.

"Feel right here for your brachioradialis," she'd say as she touched my forearm. "Now, here's the one from the model. It's a little fatter than the flexor carpi ulnaris. Can you feel the difference? Pick up the other one again." I didn't feel any difference at all; both were long, narrow arm muscles. Memorization had to be done with a functional anatomy focus, literally fleshing out the model by putting it into action in my body or in that of a classmate to feel what the muscle did.

They should have just installed a bed for me in the lab. I spent four or five hours a day assembling and dismantling those models, only leaving to go to class or to listen to more tapes in my room. Relentless is the best word to describe my study load. Sue Nelson, who was our first instructor for the practical courses in working with patients, kept reminding me, "Rely on the strengths you have, Renay. This takes much more than eyesight."

The only thing that kept me going was visualizing the patients I would someday help. *Okay, Renay, you're working with a teenager who hurt his neck playing hockey. The doctor's instructions tell you exactly which muscles need attention, and the boy is back out on the ice in no time because you studied hard; you knew what to do.*

Hopeful visions of the future kept me going. Before the first kinesiology test, I stayed through the weekend, skipping my usual time with my family. I told myself over and over that I was banking time for the future. I'd find a job right in Eau Claire. I prayed over and over, *Lord, keep me focused so that someday I can help others, so I can again be a husband with a job, a daddy that can meet the needs of my girls.*

A couple of times in those first weeks, my classmates asked me to join them for a burger or a drink. Those outings were a relief from the loneliness, but the fourth time I said, "Thanks, but I have to study."

One of my classmates replied, "So do we, but we need a break now and then."

Another laughed and added, "I have a rule that I don't spend any more time studying than breaking."

That comment made me feel so elderly that I wondered if the hair I had left was turning gray. Almost all of the other PTA students were college-aged. I reminded them, "For my job interviews in a couple years, I won't be able to refer to notes like the rest of you—I have to know this stuff off the top of my shiny head."

That first kinesiology test was during the third or fourth week of school—and I passed with an absolutely acceptable score! A few days later, my phone finally rang. "Hi, this is Pat from class," a deep male voice said. "Do you still want to join a study group? I'm thinking I need one."

Four women and one other man joined us. We met in empty classrooms, local sandwich shops, out on the campus lawn if the weather cooperated, and sometimes at someone's home.

One night, Pat and I were the only ones who showed up to eat and study. Somehow the group hadn't communicated very well, so I had enough steak from the local meat market for all seven of us and Pat had an entire grocery bag full of mushrooms from his parents' farm. I made some comment that with all of that meat on the counter it seemed like hunting season.

"You used to hunt?" Pat asked.

Pat turned out to be another outdoorsman. First he told a story about fishing on his farm, then I countered with one about an escapade with my brother. Soon we were laughing so hard that my stomach hurt. I thought, *Renay, you haven't laughed like this since the accident.*

As much as I appreciated my group's help with finding answers in their notes and the books—much faster than my having to rewind and search through tapes!—I think that I helped them as well. I'd learned all kinds of memorization techniques as I went through rehabilitation and saw ways to apply them to our coursework. Each member of the group had a special gift to pass on to the rest of us.

That study group rubbed away the sense of isolation I'd felt since I lost my sight. It was almost like being back on a crew at Cray. That spring, before one of our final exams, we all plopped down on the grass, with our feet up on a half-wall, and relaxed in the warmth of the early spring sun while we tried to come up with different sayings on how to remember muscle groups.

I knew I'd learned to fit in, despite who I was, when one day I arrived at class before anyone else—or so I thought. I settled into my chair and rested my head on my hands, thinking I had a few moments to relax, when someone hollered, "Hey, Renay!" I jolted in surprise, then hooted along with them, knowing that if my classmates could play a harmless joke on me, I was one of the gang.

Mary Sue Engman, our bubbly, animated second-year instructor, told us, "Learning is like receiving a Christmas gift, wrapped nicely in a classroom setting, which is the box, the situation that brought us all together. The gift inside is the realization of what we have and how we deal with it in our future. The teachers are the wrapping and, I believe, God and our faith comprise the ribbons and bows that tie us all together."

Mary Sue emphasized that so often what determines success in therapy is the rapport we build with patients as much as the actual therapy techniques we use. "Listen to your patients, look them in the eye, take as much time as you can to get to know each one as an individual." When we had to give an end-of the year presentation, she stated over and over, "Ten percent of your grade will be based on how you interact with the class, the eye contact you make."

I wasn't about to forfeit 10 percent of my grade, so I came up with a plan. As my presentation drew to a close, I asked, "Mary Sue, where are you sitting?"

"I'm over here," she replied.

Turning toward the sound of her voice, I tossed over a rubber eyeball Connie had purchased for me. "Is that good enough for the 10 percent of my grade?" The whole class laughed as she answered, "Oh, yes."

But I was still a hundred miles from Eau Claire. On the weekends I couldn't go home, I paced in my room, listening to study tapes, wondering if Alea had finished her bedtime storybook, what Kara chose for her bedtime snack, how tired Connie must be, whether I was foolish to spend the better part of two years away from my family.

Connie sent cards with embossed letters and raised pictures. Alea filled a tiny flowerpot with paper hearts, dried flowers, and a cotton bunny for me to feel. Kara made cards, which Pat or someone else in my study group read to me. *I love you. Do you love us? I love you, Dad.*

Just before the end of my first semester at St. Kate's, one of my study partners, Deb DeJonge, tucked a small, flat package into my hands. As I unwrapped it, she explained, "I had Connie send me a picture of your girls and I used it to embroider their faces. I hope you can use your fingers to see them now, when you're away from them."

Gently, I touched the raised outlines. Alea with shoulder-length hair. Short-haired Kara with cheeks that reminded me of Connie's. Tears came to my eyes. How do you thank someone for a present like that?

So many people helped me out and I did my best to find some way to say thank you or to help them if I could. Jerry Becker drove me to the Eau Claire–Twin Cities shuttle every week. He adored English muffin sandwiches; he didn't care whether you added bacon, ham, or sausage, as long as a slice of cheese blended everything together. So I asked Connie to help me find a recipe for homemade English muffins. The first time, I tucked some Canadian bacon in between the poached egg and the still-warm muffin halves, then wrapped it all in waxed paper. Jerry's "Oh . . . mmmmm . . . what a treat!" was all the thanks I needed.

Each bus driver I met amazed me, too. Riding to a new internship across town, I gave one driver my destination and asked him to let me know when to get off to transfer to the next bus.

A few moments later he called off the street name of the transfer point. I started to get up and the driver said, "Don't get off yet."

"Aren't we there?"

"I'm not letting you off until your next bus arrives. This is a rough corner and, well, just stay put so nothing happens to you."

How do you repay such kindness? I couldn't, really, but I thought about how I could make bus rides more enjoyable for everyone. Kitty-corner from our dorm was a small bakery. At least twice a week, I stopped in for an assortment of donuts and scones, protecting my own waistline by not getting too many jelly Bismarck's, my personal favorite. Then I passed them out to fellow passengers.

Donuts are a great way to meet people, especially those too rushed to stop for breakfast. The donuts let me start my day with an open mind about who I might meet. One December, a little girl who was all of perhaps four years of age, just like Kara, sat down next to me with her mother on the other side. "I'm Arriel," she said as she took a treat from my box. "We almost never have donuts."

I saw them several times that month, often enough to hear from Arriel that her mother had told her not to expect very much for Christmas. "Especially not the teddy bear toy I asked Santa for," she said with a sigh.

"Hush," her mother said. After a pause she murmured, "I think next year will be better for us, but. . . ." She confided to me that one night a few months before, she'd come home from work to find a U-Haul truck pulling out of her driveway. Her husband had packed up all their furniture, her clothes, their dishes and mementos, even the food in their refrigerator, leaving nothing but a note that read, "I'm outta here."

That night, I called Connie and asked her to search the Eau Claire stores for the special toy that Arriel had wished for, Teddie Ruxpin, a talking teddy bear. I only wish Connie and my girls could have heard her squeals of delight when I gave it to her the next week. Arriel's mother slipped me a thank-you card which Connie read to me later: *You showed Arriel the importance that people see from their hearts, not their eyes.* When Connie read those words aloud, I said, "It's only because so many people are using their own hearts to see what I need." As the good deeds and favors that others did for me stacked higher and higher, I found myself looking for any chance to do the same for another.

The good deeds brought back memories of Grenache's Candy Store in Superior and the generosity of the woman at the bus depot that long-ago Christmas Eve. When missing my family threatened to interfere with my schoolwork, I conjured up images of my mother, stuck in Superior from July to December without a glimpse of two of her children. She hadn't had a spouse to play with us or make our meals while she studied, or an Eau Claire Airport Shuttle to wing her back home every Friday night, or even a study group—she'd rushed right back to our little flat every day after class. If Mom had managed all of that, I could finish the physical therapy assistant program. With God's help, my faithful classmates, and the vision of what graduating would mean to my family over the next dozen years, not just the next months, I made it through.

Our original "Class of 97" dwindled from sixty to thirty-nine, but the laughter and spirit of those of us who made it pushed and pulled me into the reality of being a physical therapy assistant.

Graduation day, 1997, Connie, Kara, and Alea gathered with the friends and families of my classmates. Holding the diploma in my hand, I struggled to keep tears from falling. I had actually done it! But tears turned to shock when Mary Sue Engman, my second-year instructor, announced that my classmates had chosen me for the Outstanding Student Achievement Award. All of us had overcome so much to graduate.

In my gratitude, I composed a poem for everyone, an attempt to thank this group:

> Today is a day together we share,
> a new chapter of life, each ready to care.
> Our lives entangled, entwined into one,
> begin with a single step into the sun. . . .
> To take our blessings to patients afar,
> to share our learning, our knowledge on par. . . .
> An outstanding path we traveled in time,
> I'm honored to say we're all of a kind.
> I thank you all for being good friends,
> creating a bond that never ends.

All of my classmates had dedicated themselves to a life of caring, starting with the way each of them had cared for me, reread texts to me, marked my tapes, answered my questions, and helped me to laugh and appreciate the chance to learn together.

> When dense fog seems to hide your next step,
> have enough trust and faith in yourself to work away
> until the mist vanishes and the blue skies appear.
> The work you began in the fog will continue in the sunlight.

18

Connie and I knew that we wanted our home to be a place of love and kindness. We knew we wanted to be close to our children, and we knew that closeness depended on how we treated each other rather than the elaborateness of family vacations. Family time doesn't necessarily mean spending money or planning outings. For us, it meant finding ways to connect that strengthened our love for each other.

Family Time

GROWING UP, family time meant all six of us piling in or around our one big living room armchair in front of the little black-and-white TV.

"Gilligan's Island," the girls would cry.

Randy and I usually said, "Turn to whichever of the four channels is working best," while digging into a huge bowl of popcorn, a special treat we only had on weekends. Sometimes, we found enough pop bottles in the trash cans around town to buy pop for ourselves, too.

Family time also happened when Mom armed us each with buckets and pails for berry picking. On berry days, we didn't mind waking up early; who wanted to pick in the heat of the noonday sun? We dressed in long pants and long-sleeved shirts in a futile attempt to ward off mosquitoes and scratches from thorns.

Mom drove the old Rambler to the outskirts of town and we all tumbled out of the car to a meadow full of bushes. Within minutes, my little sisters looked like bear cubs, faces covered in red berry juice as they popped two raspberries in their mouths for every one they put in the bucket. Randy and I warned them, "The more you eat, the longer it'll take us to get enough for pies and jam!"

Occasionally, Mom, Randy, and I screamed, "Run! Bears!" to the girls, who laughed as we growled and snorted toward them.

"What love we have for each other," Mom would exclaim as we wrestled like cub bears.

Yes, we were close, but we also knew that we were different from other families in town. We'd never taken a car trip to the Black Hills like other families, not without a father to help. Mom couldn't get to our basketball and football games; she either had to work or stay home with the other children.

I grew up with very specific ideas about how active I would be in my own children's lives. *I* would be at their basketball games. *We* would drive across the country in our station wagon, seeing the Liberty Bell and Old Faithful and the great things about America. *I* would lead Cub Scouts or coach soccer or find other ways to support my children. *I* would be there for them no matter what happened.

The accident was my "no matter what." I struggled to envision how I would play my desired role in their lives. What kind of role model would I be? Would they turn to me for help? How could I be involved in their lives? The answers turned out to be more marvelous that I ever imagined.

"ONCE AGAIN, we're back at Lambeau Field, ladies and gentlemen, the home of the Green Bay Packers!" Those words meant three hours of fun at the Poiriers'. Connie was a die-hard Packers fan long before she met me. Missing a kickoff was absolutely taboo (anything you've heard about the fanaticism of "cheesehead" Packers fans is probably true).

Early on, the girls played with their dolls in the living room during the game, but they couldn't have been much more than three or four when Connie began instructing them in the basics of football. As Connie's excitement grew during a game, so did Kara and Alea's. While I listened to Z100 on the radio to get the play-by-plays, I could usually tell from my family's cheers and exclamations exactly how each play went.

Connie and Packers quarterback Brett Favre share the same birthday, October 10, another little factor in Packers fandom at our house. One year, Green Bay had a home game at Lambeau Field on October 10. I managed to acquire two precious tickets, a momentous feat in itself in this state. Then I hired a limo. Early that morning, a knock sounded at the door. Connie yelled, "Renay!" as the driver rolled out a red carpet.

"Come on, Mom," the girls shouted as they piled into the back of the limo. We drove to pick up Amber and Lynsey, a friend for each of our girls. Then we went to the park and sang "Happy Birthday" over a picnic complete with a Brett Favre cake. I handed the envelope with tickets to Connie. "You're kidding," she whispered.

"No, and I have bus tickets, too. You don't have to drive to Green Bay." Connie hugged me with a tackling lunge that would have made any Packers linebacker proud.

My mom watched the girls the rest of the day and let them stay up late to watch the game, while Connie and I boarded the bus along with dozens of other Packers fans.

Before the game started, they retired Reggie White's jersey. The two of us were standing at the railing, snapping pictures as Reggie walked by.

I hollered, "Reggie, Reggie, it's her birthday."

"Oh, my gosh, Renay, he's coming over to us!" Connie exclaimed.

Reggie gave her a happy birthday hug. That perfect day was made even better by a Packers triumph in the last twelve seconds of the game. On the bus ride home, Connie nestled into my arms and sighed, "Maybe someday we could meet Brett Favre, too."

WHEN IT WASN'T football season, country-western grabbed our attention. Eau Claire is a long way from Nashville, but we have our share of smokehouse restaurants, pick-up trucks, knee-slapping B95 music station, and music festivals—Country Fest and Country Jam.

Connie and I enjoy all kinds of music, but the whole family "went country" one afternoon as we were driving up to Grandpa and Grandma's, a country station playing over the radio. Alea was about five years old at the time. She said, "That's Tim McGraw singing 'I Like It, I Love It' " and she proceeded to sing along.

Connie said, "Where'd you learn the words?"

"Oh, I hear that one all the time," Alea said rather loftily. For the rest of the ride, Alea correctly identified the singers and their songs.

The annual June Country Music Festivals were coming up, one in Eau Claire, one in nearby Cadot. I called Randy, who lived in Texas, and asked him to send some Western outfits for the girls. Soon a box arrived filled with two white cowboy hats, blue skirts and vests with red fringe, and little red boots. As the girls squealed in delight and scurried to don the outfits, Connie said, "Oh, I wish you could see them; they could dance right up onstage in those!"

Through the years, the festival headlined the Oak Ridge Boys, Alan Jackson, Sawyer Brown, Neal McCoy, George Strait, and other family favorites. Connie's folks pulled their motor home to the festival site and we camped out for the full four days, roasting marshmallows and hot dogs over an open pit.

The first year, we sat in the handicapped area. I gave Kara and Alea turns sitting on my shoulders so they could see the stage better. Over and over we were asked, "Are they part of an act? Their outfits are so adorable!"

As country as we could be, loving every moment, a dream came true when two elderly ladies gave their backstage passes to Alea and Kara. Tim McGraw and Faith Hill invited Kara and Alea backstage and had pictures taken with the girls. That happened year after year, artist after artist. Their music and actions clearly spelled out a love of country—and a country full of love.

While Avril Lavigne, O-Town, and the Backstreet Boys eventually supplemented country fare, the girls still consider the festivals a mandatory family vacation.

"LET'S GO TO the Blugold basketball game tonight," Connie announced one Saturday when Alea was nine and Kara was six. "The girls will love the noise and excitement, and they've got a good team this year." A University of Eau Claire graduate, Connie always enjoyed the school's Blugold basketball team. I became a Blugold, too, when I took several summer classes there in conjunction with my program at St. Kate's.

Connie found some blue and gold caps and T-shirts for the girls to wear, along with pom-poms from the university store. I brought along my radio so I could follow the play-by-play without Connie having to stop cheering to describe every basket. We held hands, yelling with excitement each time the team scored.

As we walked out that night, Alea asked, "When's the next game?"

We made it to every single men's home game and soon started attending the women's games, too. We usually got there early enough to sit right across from the Blugold players' bench, at half-court. At tournament time, we went so far as to paint our faces blue and yellow, which gained the girls a spot on television one year.

Such devotion from two little girls caught the attention of the coach and soon our girls were the honorary "water girls" for the team. They filled little cups for the players from the big yellow thermos during the games. During warmups and halftime, they handed out basketballs and put them away again. And every year we were invited to the Blugold Banquet. One year the girls brought little beribboned bottles of water for each player, with a gallon jug for Andy Witte, the 6'8" player who hustled like no other player, and, no surprise, drank the most water during the season!

Part of our Blugold tradition was helping the girls learn the Star-Spangled Banner. We taught them phrase by phrase, adding a few words every night, until they could join in the singing at each game, building community and a family, thanks to the big-hearted Blugold players and coaches.

BEANIE BABIES as quality time? While we never succumbed to paying outrageous sums for six ounces of fur and pellets, my years at St. Kate's were during the height of the Beanie Baby rage. Our family started simply enough, a tiny five-dollar animal tucked into each girl's Christmas stocking. In the days that followed, Kara and Alea found all kinds of games to play with the little things—and with their detailed ears, whiskers, and wings, it was easy for me to tell which was which.

I started bringing one or two home with me on the weekends, and suddenly, we were collectors. Kara or Alea described new ones to me in great detail and helped me memorize its birthday, which was printed on its little red tag. Those little creatures gave me something to touch, feel, and share with the girls.

AN EVEN MORE important kind of sharing took place when we found ways to serve together. Sometimes we discussed where we would donate some money, or we'd "adopt" a family and go Christmas shopping for them. We rang bells for the Salvation Army, staffed the church nursery, acted as hosts for homeless families, and helped with the children's liturgy time.

Connie and I constantly sought opportunities for service that were also family outings. I'll never forget one fishing expedition. Two of my patients were twin girls, about Kara and Alea's age. Both were wheelchair bound, but only in body, not spirit. One day as I worked with them, I learned that they'd never been fishing. "Well, we'll have to fix that," I told them.

Their mother thought it was a wonderful idea. Connie, the girls, and I packed up our van with poles, bait, chairs, and picnic supplies, then picked up the twins and drove to a trout pond. Kara and Alea set up lawn chairs for them, then guided me as I carried each of the twins about seventy-five yards past a little creek, over hill and dale, to our fishing hole. Connie and I listened with delight as Kara and Alea baited hooks for the girls, helped bring the fish in, and displayed the kind of patience and joy in helping that we'd always hoped they would have. High-pitched giggles and screams filled the air when the twins held the slimy fish for a photograph.

EVENTUALLY, we even embarked on a car trip, the kind of vacation that had loomed so large in my vision of family life. Some dear friends, Brett and Amy, had moved from Eau Claire to Laramie, Wyoming. Connie said, "We'll make that trip to the Black Hills you've always wanted to do, then spend some time with Brett and Amy."

"That's too much driving for you," I said. "It just wouldn't be fair."

"I'll manage this once," Connie replied. "After all, the girls are older now. They're great travelers. And, if it goes well, we'll be able to take other trips in summers to come."

Reluctantly, I agreed. Not being able to drive was still one of my biggest feelings of loss.

But what a trip it was. We took a horseback ride at a campground at Mt. Rushmore. The kind folks helped me mount my steady steed. The horses were trained to follow each other, but I had visions of snakes scaring my horse over a cliff, even of cougars making lunchmeat of my children. I shook off my fears and had a beautiful time. The man who owned the horses was in his early eighties, but he still went on every ride. When he found out it was Kara's birthday, he chased her across the fields to give her a "cowboy kiss," a whisker rub—and was limber enough to catch her. We ate pork and beans out of a skillet up in the mountains, like the cowboys.

We also stopped at Wind Cave. At one point in the tour, our guide got us all nestled into chairs, said, "Hold a hand next to you," then turned off all the lights in the cavern. As my eyes fought to adjust to that total darkness, screams echoed around me. I thought, *Renay, there is still so much light in your life. Although you can't see, you're a far cry from total darkness—with family, with a new career, with a future, there's plenty to see.*

Our four days in Wyoming with Brett and Amy were a magical time of reminiscing, exploring, and relaxation. Brett said, "Let's try out your casting at the town fishpond. Depending on what you think, we could head into the mountains tomorrow."

Twenty-four hours later, Brett was guiding me through the brush to his secret spot, "where you won't have to worry about snagging anyone, Renay. Not that I'm worried, you hit the water every time in town." Fly-fishing was in my blood—Grandpa Meier had drilled Randy and me until we could cast a fly into a coffee can at seventeen paces.

I knew I wouldn't catch anything; I seemed to find every rock and log around us with my lures. But I was every inch a contented fisherman, standing in the ice-cold water, listening to the rushing stream and the wind dancing around the leaves in the trees above us.

Suddenly, I felt that familiar pull, those defining, rhythmic tugs from the jaws of a trout pulsing through the line to my fingers, straight to the heart of the fisherman I'd always been. *Wait, wait, now!* I told myself as I jerked to set the hook. The fish fought back gloriously, letting me revel in the thrill of the moment.

As I released the fish, I must have thanked my friend a thousand times. In my darkness, the beauty of God shined brightly through faith and hope, but, most importantly, through countless acts of kindness, in love.

On our third day with our friends, Connie confided how incredible the strain of doing all the driving had been. "I don't know how I can possibly drive all the way home. I'm just plain exhausted."

That night as I gently stroked the hair from her temples, I whispered, "Just four more hours of driving, honey."

"You're confused, it's at least twenty hours back to Eau Claire."

"No, I've got a surprise, and I think it's time to let you in on it. Uncle Gary's flying in to Denver to meet us. He and I will drive the van back, you and the girls are flying home. Love you, dear."

"Oh, I love you, babe," she said with a big hug, then fell into a deep slumber.

Affection, respect, patience, forgiveness, encouragement, love . . . you don't have to be able to see, you don't have to be rich, you don't have to be smart to provide all those things to your children. Families are a work of art from the heart, filled with the colors of emotion. As the years wore on, full of memory-building family time, I began to relax and enjoy my children's creativity, trusting that Beanie Babies and Blugold games were bonding us together. We were a family.

Each day well lived makes every yesterday a dream of happiness and each tomorrow a vision of hope.

19

Grandpa Meier had a saying, "Things can never be so bad that they can't get worse." At times while attending St. Kate's, I felt like I was living out that saying. Loneliness nearly pulled me back into the trap of feeling useless. While I was moving toward a better future, I felt as if I was letting my family down, perhaps jeopardizing our future.

Then another dose of trouble seized my attention, taking my focus off of my own woes. I refocused on what was really important: God and family.

A Whisper from Heaven

LIKE MOST CHILDREN, our girls loved to watch home videos of themselves. I loved hearing their voices and imagining what the scenes of birthdays and holidays must have been like. But one night, as the tape of Alea's third birthday played, a nagging fear in the back of my mind grew louder and louder. My memory wasn't distorted; Alea at age three was using full sentences, trying out big words, asking questions constantly. Kara was almost three, yet she barely ever talked. Was there something wrong?

Child-rearing experts warn parents not to compare their children to each other, or to anyone else's children, but the contrast was too stark to ignore. Kara said "Eea" for Alea, "Yaya" for her Aunt Shelley. One day I said, "Come here, Kara" and she brought me the cat's brush, thinking I'd said, "Comb hair."

Then our sitter confided, "I'm worried about Kara. Often, she sits alone on the couch for most of the day."

We set up an appointment with our pediatrician. He confirmed our suspicions: Kara had significant hearing loss. A trip to a specialist revealed that the tiny bones in her ears, the hammer, anvil, and stirrup, were somewhat fused together, preventing the vibrations that allow us to hear. She'd been born that way.

The doctors recommended that we immediately enroll Kara in speech therapy classes for children with hearing impairment. There was a special preschool in our town. "We can also do surgery. In fact, freeing up the anvil and hammer while she's so young will give her the best chance of developing normal speech patterns."

But the risks were high—sometimes facial nerves were cut in the process. Kara might end up with droopy eyelids or a crooked mouth distorting her little face.

As we agonized over the doctor's words, Connie described Kara's little pixie cheeks to me for the thousandth time, her sparkling dark eyes, and the smile that spread from chin to forehead when she was happy. "I . . . how can we make a decision that could harm her? Can she thrive with hearing aids?"

I felt like a character in a horror picture, where they slow down the action at the most frightening moment. Connie and I couldn't eat, couldn't sleep. We were still trying to get on our feet after my accident; how could calamity strike us again so soon? In despair, I asked Connie, "What else can go wrong for us?"

We decided to drive the two hundred miles to Rochester's Mayo Clinic for a second opinion, leaving at dawn with our two sleepy girls nodding in the backseat. As we drove, Connie and I attempted to talk about the garden and the weather, but our thoughts focused on prayer. *Not Kara, too, God . . . I'd rather be deaf and blind than have her go through anything. I'd give myself a hundred times over.*

If the reason for our visit hadn't been so serious, the day would have been a great family outing. The doctors let Alea hop right up on the table with Kara, showed her what they were doing, and let her "help" by imitating their gestures and holding Kara's hand. Alea said, "I feel like a doctor."

For one of the tests, Kara sat inside a little room, wearing headphones, while Connie, Alea, and I sat outside its sound-proof glass. I wondered if Kara felt isolated like that in everyday living. Kara was supposed to signal whether she heard tones in her left or right ear. The doctors noted her reactions, but suddenly started laughing. "What's going on?" I whispered to Connie.

"Kara and Alea are making faces at each other through the glass. Kara's really having fun."

The doctors explained everything first in terms Connie and I could understand, then to Kara and Alea. With a sucker or two in hand, the girls pronounced the Mayo Clinic a fine place. But the doctors' prognosis was the same—hearing aids or the surgery.

Connie and I prayed for guidance. The surgical risks were too high. "If she opts for the surgery when she's eighteen, it'll be her decision, not ours. And maybe technology will improve. But I can't make a decision that could rob Kara of her smile," I told Connie. She squeezed my hand in agreement.

We had Kara fitted for hearing aids. At first, getting them adjusted and in place each morning was like trying to ride a Brahman bull. Kara tugged at them, whined, scratched, and scowled, "No, no," one of her clearest words. Sometimes she complained that they whistled in her ears, too.

Attending the preschool helped, for there Kara wasn't the only one with hearing aids. Gradually, she discovered how much more she could hear while wearing them. She stopped fighting us, but waited each day for Connie or me to help her put them in before breakfast.

Our hearts melted in thankfulness as Kara's speech improved. Now that she could hear the voices of other children, Kara blossomed. Her preschool teacher, Linda, told us how Kara loved to help the younger children, showing them things she had learned, and taking them by the hand to lead them to new places in the building. We trusted that our decision had been right. Kara's shining spirit told me that she was doing fine without the surgery.

Sometimes Kara would ask, "Why do I have to wear these? Do I look funny?"

"Aren't you glad there are hearing aids?" I asked, trying to encourage her. "What if we didn't have anything to help you?"

Kara was silent for a moment, then said softly, "I wish there were seeing aids, Daddy."

I hugged her. If Kara was to keep her sweet spirit in spite of her hearing problems, I had to act as if I didn't mind not being able to see. "Oh, but I'm thankful for my cane, and tape recorders, the new stove, and my two girls who are always willing to help me—I have so many seeing aids. We'll say a prayer of thanks when we put the batteries in your hearing aids each morning, okay?"

The box that held Kara's hearing aids would have been fun if its purpose wasn't so serious. The small plastic container had three drawers: the left hearing aid went in the top drawer, the right in the middle, and the batteries in the bottom. To avoid corrosion, we popped out the batteries each night.

Then each morning, I'd sneak into Kara's room, quietly push the buttons that opened each drawer, and insert the batteries. They were tiny, a challenge even for a person with 20/20 vision, but I could feel the ridge that let me tell positive from negative. Usually, as I fussed with the aids, Kara awoke and greeted me with a hug.

While we certainly kept wishing and praying that Kara's hearing would improve, the difference that the hearing aids made let us know that our daughter would be fine. One morning, Kara's teacher called. "Kara and some of the other children have a chance to be part of a television program."

That day at the TV station convinced us that that we'd been right in avoiding surgery for Kara. For fifteen to twenty minutes, six children from Kara's school talked about using hearing aids and audio amplifiers in the classroom. They loved being in the limelight, all of them up on their knees around a table. Anxious as they were to share their own stories, they gave their full attention to each child, listening intently to each child's triumphs and struggles.

Yet as I started school at St. Kate's, the shadow of Kara's hearing problems engulfed the entire family and encouraged us to grow closer. Working with Kara took extra time, and now I wasn't around to help Connie. We always had to face Kara, speak more slowly and a little louder, often adding gestures to show her what we wanted to do. Part of me kept saying, *You should have found a way to stay in Eau Claire. You'll never finish this program; a third of each class drops out, why will you be different? You're wasting time that you could use to help at home. You're just letting everybody down. . . .*

I'm not sure how long I might have wallowed in self-pity, alone in my dorm room, if our study group hadn't started. At first we were all business—preparing for anatomy tests took up what little time we had together. But gradually, we shared bits and pieces of our personal lives. Mixa Patel and I became great friends. She was from India and I could understand her accent better than anyone else. Pat Schmidt still missed the quiet of his parents' farm. And Terry Bohmbach, well, when I learned she commuted three hours a day from Red Wing, Minnesota, to attend classes, I felt a little guilty about the extra study time staying at the dorms afforded me. When I found out that she was a single mother of five daughters, the youngest of whom was only eight, my self-pity took a good kick to the ribs. Who was I to complain?

One day, as we swapped stories about our children, she said, "Renay, we're both parents doing the best we can so our children can have the best future we can give them. Though miles apart, we could never be separated. The family's heart beats as one."

Still, I struggled to turn off worries about the bills and about how hard Connie was working and about Kara's hearing and about my future. On my weekends home, I clung to my girls, wishing I could be with them all the time, wondering if being at St. Kate's was truly what God wanted me to do.

Those Saturdays at home, I resumed all of my normal responsibilities, delighting in helping Connie with baths, story time, making three meals a day. My time with the girls often started with fixing Kara's hearing aids as soon as I heard her stirring.

One morning, I gently opened her door, tiptoed toward her dresser, and softly pushed the buttons on the little drawers. I planned to awaken Kara with a kiss as soon as I had both aids working properly. As I fumbled with the tiny batteries, I heard Kara yawn, then say, "Daddy, I can hear you."

"Oh, I'm sorry," I said, loudly as usual, walking over to where she could see my lips. "Did I bump the dresser too hard?"

"No, Daddy, I can hear you talking. I won't need the hearing aids today."

"Kara, you know you wear them every day."

"Daddy, I can hear you. I don't need them."

I assumed she was joking, but I said, "Stay in here while I get something from the living room." I walked out her door and a few feet down the hall, then said in a normal tone, "Kara, come to Daddy."

In an instant, her little feet scampered across the carpet. "What do you need?"

"Ah, go tell Mommy I want to talk to her." Off she went as I stood there dumbfounded. Connie soon came out of our bedroom and I murmured, "Kara says she can hear me, and the aids are still on her dresser."

"Honey, did you want pancakes for breakfast?" Connie whispered.

"Oh, Mommy, that's my favorite. With lots of syrup!" Kara said, her laughter ringing with the sound of heaven's angels all around. "And I can hear you."

The hearing aids still sit on a table beside our bed. The doctors tested Kara's ears and agreed that she could now hear adequately without them. They didn't understand why; the bones in her ears were still partially fused together. A miracle? Perhaps not in a medical sense, for she still has some measure of hearing loss. However, something definitely changed; she no longer needs the hearing aids.

Able to hear on her own, Kara's joyful spirit flourished even more. She thrived on excitement, trying new things.

Connie said, "Her delightful smile is enough to warm the coldest of hearts and the saddest of eyes."

Now when Kara kicks the soccer ball into a goal or makes a basket playing basketball, she doesn't have to wonder if we're cheering. She can hear her family with joys of support ringing out a joyous tune, "Go, Kara, go!"

What could I say in the face of such overwhelming evidence that God was still with us? Who was I to worry about my future when I still had my family, held together by our love of Jesus and each other? As I tried to grasp the enormity of all of the blessings in our lives, I think God smiled. *Renay, stop thinking that you have to be in charge. I'm here, now you do your part by just doing your best. And let others know how much I care.*

I am weak, foolish, selfish, lacking in faith
and commitment, until once again
God reminds me that he is with us always.

20

My years at St. Kate's ended with several internships: at a children's hospital, a rehabilitation center, long-term care, acute care — a wide variety of arenas that gave us a taste of the kinds of settings in which we could choose to work.

For me to be comfortable with patients, I needed more help than the average rookie. At every place I interned, thoughtful supervisors mapped out the work areas for me and assisted in marking my equipment. Occasionally, though, a sigh or a clipped response revealed a belief that I was being too demanding.

Sacred Heart Hospital in Eau Claire was the site of my last internship. My direct supervisors, Kay, Beth, and Judy, seemed to assume that their time with me was an investment, speeding my way to self-sufficiency. At Sacred Heart, I felt as if God had rolled out a red carpet for me. I truly felt at home.

A Perfect Fit

THE ELEVATOR BELL sounded as I checked the time on my talking watch. I was early. Good. This was my first morning at Sacred Heart and I longed to make a good impression. I felt the Braille symbols alongside the floor buttons. There, that was number 9. For the most part Braille was a mystery to me, but knowing the numbers came in handy. The doors closed and I was on my way.

"You must be Renay," a voice greeted me as I pushed open the department doors for the first time. A woman shook my hand and said, "I'm Kay, one of your supervisors. You'll be glad to know that someone from St. Kate's was here yesterday. I think they did a marvelous job marking everything for you—raised dots on the machines, knotted strings on the weights to indicate the poundage. Would you feel comfortable exploring on your own for just a minute or two?"

The warmth in her voice relaxed me as she guided me toward one of the stations. I picked up one of the weights and felt for the knots, wondering what this internship would be like. *Send someone to help me, Lord, so that I quickly become an extra pair of hands and not a burden.*

More voices filled the room, then footsteps sounded toward me. "Renay, if you'll come this way—I mean, walk toward, um, 3 o'clock," Kay said. "The three of us would like to meet with you before the day begins."

Beth and Judy introduced themselves to me. "We'll team together to help you," they said.

Judy added, "We know it'll take most of the day for you to get oriented. I'll stay with you as long as you need to get this place mapped out in your mind. I'll show you where the equipment is now. We can organize it together for you."

"And there's a lull in my patient load this afternoon," said Beth, "so I can go through procedures with you then."

The morning rushed by as Judy helped me pace off the distances between the different therapy stations and memorize the locations where equipment was stored. Before lunch, she asked me to gather a few items for a patient session. "Already you show such confidence as you walk around the department," she told me. I tried not to laugh as I thanked her for the compliment; actually, I'd banged my shins against a table leg.

Not once during the entire internship, did Kay, Beth, or Judy sigh at my endless questions or answer impatiently. They often left taped instructions for me so I could familiarize myself with a patient's history and treatment plan. I couldn't afford to rely on just my memory; I had to get things right for each person I worked with. Once, I said, "Sorry to bother you with another question, but. . . ."

"Renay, you're never a bother," Kay stopped me. "The time I spend now is like an investment for the future. I want you to be confident in your work."

Their taped instructions contained a mix of information, professional guidance, and tender care. If a patient needed a treatment that was still rather new to me, Kay added a comment like, "Not to worry, Renay, just be yourself."

Or when a patient needed help walking, Beth reminded me, "Ask the patient for help or for more background information. Keep smiling and keep focused on the patient's goals." Clearly, it took more effort to train me, yet every word, every gesture from them said to me, *We want you here. You can do good work.*

Much later, Bob Green, the physical therapy director at Sacred Heart, told me, "My greatest fear was that you'd fall downstairs while working with a patient—and take the patient down with you! But I kept telling myself that I worry too much about every employee, I lose way too much sleep over things better left to prayer."

During the last week of my internship, Bob asked me, "What specialty are you considering?"

"Children," I replied.

"Oh, we have enough therapists in that area right now."

"Children of God, I mean."

After a moment's silence, Bob said, "Wow, leave a copy of your résumé with me. As soon as you graduate, give me first chance at hiring you."

My heart did a double flip as I walked out of his office. I hadn't planned the children of God statement; it came straight from my heart. Yes, I hoped to work at Sacred Heart. I'd be so close to home. The staff accepted me as a person. Most important, though, as an employee of a Catholic hospital, I could speak openly about prayer and faith with my patients. The hospital's literature states:

> *The primary motive of our ministry is to reveal and embody Christ's healing love to all people. There are three things that last forever: faith, hope love, but the greatest of them all is love. We at Sacred Heart Hospital join together to promote personal and professional growth to keep alive the ideals of healing as Jesus did, knowing that his love heals.*

BEING A PART of that ministry would fulfill my dreams of helping others in a manner more complete than I'd even imagined.

After graduation, I took the national board exams as quickly as I could, then worked with the placement office at St. Kate's to find a permanent position. I had offers from several of the places I interned, but I didn't see how I could work in Minneapolis or Hudson. Even in Eau Claire, my options were limited to locations along the bus routes. How else would I get to work day after day?

Then Sacred Heart called me for another interview. Bob and I talked through the special needs I had for work and he agreed that everything could be handled easily. I was hired on September 2, 1997.

From my first moments on the floor, I felt at home. My supervisors, Kay and Beth, met with me. Patiently, kindly, wisely, they explained the types of patients I'd be seeing at first, how we'd start each day, how to ask for help. They walked me through the physical therapy department again: "This is where you'll greet patients; here are our offices; we'll leave your tapes in this basket each night so you'll have them first thing in the morning."

I designed a special holster to hold my cane and my goniometer, a device that measures joint range of motion. Connie, Kara, and Alea had helped me adapt one for people with visual impairments; it worked so well that we made several and shipped them to St. Kate's for other students.

I kept my Scriptwriter close at hand, an easy way to pass notes on each patient to Kay and Beth at the end of the day. There were also productivity reports to complete, as well as scheduling systems. I hadn't had to do much paperwork as an intern. I must have looked a bit panicky, for Kay gave my arm a pat and said, "Don't let anything get you down. You were hired because you already showed us that you can do the job."

That first day of being fully in charge of patients had me shaking emotionally if not physically. What if I grabbed the wrong equipment or the wrong patient or the wrong affected area of the patient? What if I went to the wrong place? I told myself, *Renay, get a grip. Kay trusts you enough to let you be on your own; now trust yourself.*

One of my first patients was an older man named Armond. I'm well over six-feet tall, and strong, but Armond was at least six-feet-four and probably over 250 pounds, a mountain of a man. He'd had a stroke and told me, "I'll do anything to walk again. Work me as hard as you can . . . but it's tough for me to not be afraid of falling. The ground's a long way down!"

I said, "Well, I've got the muscles, you've got the eyes. Let's form a partnership."

"You really can't see, can you?" he asked. "Well, I guess if you can do all this, I can certainly try to put one foot in front of the other."

I got underneath his arm, asking him to tell me what he saw on the other side of the room. We figured out a course and began. I said, "I'll be telling you at almost every step where you need to shift your weight or adjust your stride. Don't make your steps too big, just work on a straight line."

I forced myself to concentrate on the sound of Armond's breathing, on any extra little movements that might indicate exhaustion or loss of balance, and on keeping a soft, encouraging tone in my instructions. When we made it to the other side, I think we both had tears in our eyes. It was the first time he'd walked since the stroke. As we finished the session, he said, "Renay, I felt like the center of your universe as you worked with me. While all of the employees here are nice, working with you gave me a shot of confidence."

"I was thinking the same thing about you," I said through the lump in my throat that had formed in our triumph.

Maybe that's my God-given strength, I thought. The concentration I exert because I can't see lets me hear and feel things that others don't. My lack of sight didn't mean I would never be an excellent physical therapy assistant; I could strive to be excellent in my own way.

Self-doubt didn't disappear overnight, but my experiences with specific patients the following weeks chipped it away bit by bit.

Some patients gave me the gift of laughter. I asked one patient to warn me of any obstacles as I wheeled her toward my station. She said, "You really can't see me? And here I was all worried because I hadn't washed and curled my hair before physical therapy. It has to be a terrible sight!"

I explained, "I've lost interest in judging people, anyway—it's more fun to be overwhelmed in appreciating others just the way they are!"

I wasn't being flippant. It was true. By this point I'd been judged by so many people that I knew better than to listen to their opinions. For example, one day I had to ask Kay to read me something from a patient's chart. The patient muttered, "He doesn't know how to read?"

Kay explained my situation to him.

One of my patients, a priest who'd taken a bad fall, seemed almost oblivious to his aches and his serious heart condition. As I helped him with some gentle exercises, he said, "Take your cane and slap it against the mat as hard as you can."

So I pulled my cane out of my holster, extended it out, and slapped it. It echoed through the whole ninth floor of the hospital. The priest cried, "Aaaaagh," then whispered, "Again." CRACK. "Aaaaagh." Nurses came running from everywhere and he laughed and laughed. "You should see your faces. Oh, I haven't played a good practical joke in years," he chortled. Then, having a captive audience, he continued, "I've been thinking about starting a new drive-through confessional, called 'Toot and Tell or Go to Hell!' "

This priest who was young and old at the same time seemed to have an uncontrollable urge to extend the love and blessings given to him; I felt the same way. I think we shared the belief I'd once heard, "Work hard, go a hundred smiles an hour, and your day will be great."

Laughter lessened my fears about making little mistakes. I walked into the wrong patients' rooms enough times, no matter how carefully I planned, that I learned to say, "Sorry, I lost my sheep. Some shepherd, huh?" Then I'd sing on the way out, "Oh when the saints, go marching in. . . ." I guess

I started to act more spontaneously instead of basing my actions on fears from past experiences.

My confidence grew as I developed more and more ways of compensating for my lack of sight. The supervisors let me use neon tape to mark the ward floor. That way, I could tell if my patients were walking in a straight line. I designed and built a special equipment rack, as well as holders for the giant exercise balls. The fewer things on the floors, the better for our patients and for me!

After a few months Kay told me, "You keep the rest of us on our toes about keeping the area clutter-free. That is a really good thing." Eventually, Kay trusted my ability to fix things and began to rely on me for repairing wheelchair brakes and pedal adjustments.

Getting to work, though, loomed as difficult a task as memorizing bones and muscles had been. I planned to use city transit and taxis as much as I could, but sometimes I needed a ride—to get home earlier because of Connie's schedule or for meetings at work or any number of other things. I hated asking for favors; once I had to call twenty friends and fellow employees before I found a ride.

And there was no perfect formula for asking. If I said, "I'll gladly pay you," some thanked me while others accused me of being ungrateful. If I only gave verbal thank-you's, others made it clear how inconvenient it was to shuttle me around. I had nightmares about being late to work and about offending every last person I knew!

Kathy Woodford worked as an aide in the physical therapy department. Her husband, Jerry Sr., had helped me get my first electrician job in Eau Claire. I'd roomed with Jerry Jr. when I first moved to town and was best man for his wedding. One morning Kathy announced, "From now on, we're your ride."

While I occasionally still rode the bus, Jerry and Kathy seldom let me! Even if they had the day off, they usually showed up at my door despite my protests. "It's what we want to do for you; don't worry." I know that Jerry loved to talk with me about our days as electricians. Arthritis had forced him into early retirement and he missed his work as much as I had until my new career was underway.

One of my longer-term patients was a teenager named Christy. She was a great piano player and full of spirit, but surgery for a brain tumor had robbed her of the motor skills she needed to walk. Even though she was told there wasn't much of a chance, she poured her heart into every session with me.

I think all of us poured our hearts into helping Christy. At night at home, I tried out new movements on myself to see if they would use the right muscles. Kay, Beth, and I conferred, improvised, and brainstormed for ways to help her. At every session, Christy repeated, "I just want to walk." Occasionally, after a really tough session, I made sure I had a Beanie Baby or other little gift for her the next time, a small way of showing that we cared.

It took months, but Christy learned to walk without walkers or crutches or any device. Those were the moments that made our work a privilege.

For the longest time, though, I struggled to believe that I could do my job as well as anyone else could. When I received a Sunshine Employee Award during my first month at Sacred Heart, I felt proud, but at the same time I wondered if I could continue to achieve success through positive patient care. My white cane and sunglasses didn't stand between me and my task of helping others, but I had so much more to learn.

Kay told me, "You're an asset to the department. At least a dozen patients have said, 'If Renay overcame his disability, then I can work hard to overcome mine as well.' "

"Not everyone looks at me that way, though," I replied. "Sometimes I'm lucky not to be able to see the expressions on people's faces." We both laughed, recalling Ray McFarlane.

Ray was in his mid-seventies when he suffered a stroke. Six months after he finished physical therapy sessions, he came back to visit me and confessed, "Renay, the morning I met you I was in a world of hurt. I was stuck in a wheelchair, gripping the armrests to keep from complaining. A part of me was wondering if my life was pretty much over. But I kept telling myself, 'No pain, no gain. You're going to put every effort into therapy.'

"And what happens next? A man comes out waving a white cane and says, 'Hi, I'm here to help teach you to walk.' I thought, *The odds are against me. It can't get worse.* I almost tried to get up and run away!"

I laughed, remembering that there'd been quite a pause before he shook my hand that morning. "I suppose I am a rather scary sight."

"Yeah, I just about flipped out of my wheelchair. But I was wrong, Renay. You made me feel as if we were on a team together, a team with the sole goal of making me walk again."

On that dark day that found me hovering by the river, my mother had said, "Renay, God has work for you. You've got to find a way to help people." At Sacred Heart, I found what God had in mind.

*Institutions, like vineyards, should be judged
by the quality of their vintages!*

21

Until it happens, our human spirits can't comprehend how quickly one event can change the course of our lives. I knew; it had happened to me. The more I worked with patients, the more I saw how my own experiences built a bridge toward people in need of not just physical but spiritual healing.

Split-Second Changes

"YOU CAN PROBABLY scratch Dorothy Eslinger from your patient list today, Renay," Kay told me. "She's having a rough morning, and who can blame her?"

We all knew of Dorothy. Only a week had passed since she discovered her husband dead, then fell to the floor herself with a ruptured aneurysm as she dialed 911.

I'd already listened to the instruction tape for Dorothy several times; she was one of the first patients for whom I had full responsibility. I checked my watch; my next patient wasn't for a full hour, so I decided to pay a visit to Mrs. Eslinger. It might help me plan for her session the next day.

As I walked toward her room, my mind pondered how quickly things happen. A bundle of wires that should have been dead, a tug, an explosion of light—and my life changed in a split second. *Lord*, I prayed, *she must be so confused. What can I say to her?* I knocked quietly, hearing the gentle sound of her crying even through the door.

"Mrs. Eslinger, dear, what's going on? What can I help you with?" I said as I felt for a chair beside her bed. "I'm Renay Poirier, the physical therapy assistant assigned to you."

A quavery voice said, "But I'll never walk again; there's no use going on, I'm of no use to anyone. I'll never live in my home again. Howard—yesterday, I couldn't even attend his funeral."

I reached for her hand. "Do you want to talk about it?"

"I suppose I should, since none of it seems real yet. Howard was, well, that morning we'd had just a bit of snow. I awoke before Howard and swept off the front porch before collecting the newspaper. I thought I heard him stir, so I went in to ask him if he wanted some breakfast. He said, 'I'm not quite awake yet. Can I sleep just a bit longer?'

"I tiptoed out, swept off the back porch, then fixed his favorite breakfast—eggs, toast, and juice. I dished up everything but the eggs and headed back to call Howard. I remember being puzzled that the aroma of eggs hadn't brought him to the kitchen, but I never imagined. . . . The instant I opened the bedroom door, I knew something was wrong. When he didn't respond to my hug, I felt for a pulse and then grabbed for the phone and dialed 911. Then I called our daughter. That's all I remember."

I gave her hand a squeeze and said, "How awful, how lonely."

"Our son told me he thought he'd be planning a double funeral, what with my being in surgery for ten hours. Oh, why didn't I just die, too?" Her voice broke off in a muffled wail.

By this time tears were streaming down my face as well. "Mrs. Eslinger, there was a time when I wanted to die, too. But I still had a wife, my girls—think if your children had really lost both of you at once."

"Why? What happened?" As I quickly told of my accident, Dorothy sobbed even harder. Just then the door opened. "Renay, what's going on?" my supervisor exclaimed.

I cleared my throat, thinking of how unimpressive our exchange must seem. "Dorothy needed someone to hear her story, and I thought it would help us set some goals for therapy."

"All right," she said with a note of doubt in her voice as she left us alone again.

"Dorothy," I continued, "God still wants you here for a reason."

"Well, I don't know what it would be if I can't get out of bed to talk with people."

"Maybe that's the goal, to help you learn to use a wheelchair, maybe even a powered one."

She was silent for a moment. "My son is looking into retirement homes for me. Maybe I'd enjoy living around lots of people if I can get out and talk with them."

"There you are," I said.

Day after day we worked together. At first, she struggled even to move from the bed to a wheelchair. "This is step one toward your new life as a visiting ray of sunshine," I told her, which made her laugh.

Often, Dorothy wanted to speak of the pain of missing her husband's funeral and feeling robbed of the chance to say good-bye. Then one day she said, "I can tell you things because your life changed in a split second, too. Yet you went on."

"Dorothy, it took me *years* to go on. You're an inspiration to me as you work so hard to regain your strength."

"That's only because you're an inspiration to *me*." Then she revealed that on that first day, when we'd cried together, she thought I'd made up the story of my accident to make her feel better. "Another therapist set me straight. I'm so sorry."

"No need to apologize, some days I can't believe I'm a physical therapy assistant, either."

SO MANY of my patients' lives had changed in a split second. Often, their bodies seemed to heal faster than their spirits and they needed to pour out their stories. Telling my own story made phrases like "I understand" or "I know how it feels" ring with authenticity, providing light to those who perceived only darkness ahead.

Not every patient wanted or needed to hear of my past troubles, though, so I constantly worried about whether I'd choose the right times to share. Would I find a way to each patient's heart to help them? I could only try.

Sometimes, all I had to do was listen. One elderly farmer still sighed in disbelief over what had happened to him. "I've tended cattle my whole life. My brother and I just keep twenty head or so, now. We decided to care for the farm together after my wife died. So, last Saturday started like any other. I went out to throw a couple of bales of hay into the pasture while my brother made breakfast.

"I stepped through the gate to check for water in the tank, like I've done thousands of times before, and this heifer butts into me, knocks me right to the ground, then starts trampling me. I crawled for the fence, but he butted me back again. I thought I was done for, even saw a bright light coming toward me, when my brother came running toward the animal with a pitchfork.

"The animal turned on him, too, but I rolled toward the fence, screaming, and he had just enough time to get out."

"Wow, is your brother okay?"

"Yep, but the heifer isn't. He's hamburger now and we're going to smile with every bite." He paused for a minute. "I think we're done farming. We'd best fold the place. Funny how fast life changes, isn't it, when it seems like things will stay the same forever?"

How well I knew.

WHILE I CONCENTRATED on helping every patient, some I'll never forget. The first time that I met Millie Edie, a stroke victim who was ninety years old, Kay had already been working with him for several days. One morning I sensed that Kay was in tears. When I asked if she was okay, she told me, "It's Millie. He's given up. It's the first time I've had a patient tell me, 'Please, just let me die. I'm of no use in this world any longer.'"

I know how that feels, I thought to myself. That evening, I slipped into Millie's room after work was over. His wife said, "His eyes are closed, his face is turned from the door." I sat down and touched his hand. "Mr. Edie," I said. "I'm Renay Poirier, one of the physical therapy assistants. I hear you had a rough day."

I heard him sigh, but he didn't respond, so I continued. "I'm glad your wife came by. You're so lucky to be able to see her every day. You know. . . ." I told him what had happened to me. "I still miss being able to see my children. You have so much to be thankful for."

We talked about his life, his wife and children, and I said, "Think of all that you have. That's what life's about." Finally, Millie seemed to be dozing off, so I got up and left quietly, with a prayer that he'd try life again.

The next morning, Kay came up to me and said, "Renay, what did you say to Millie?" She sounded all excited and I thought I must have done something wrong.

I said, "I only talked with him for a bit last night."

"Well, I wish we had your words on tape. You'll never guess—he was sitting on his bed, dressed, ready to go. He wants to work. He told me, 'If Renay didn't give up, I guess I can't either.'"

I started working with Millie the next day. He was quite frail and I wanted to build his confidence that his efforts would be worth it. One of my other patients for the day was a little girl, perhaps five or six years old, who had suffered burns to her arms. I said to Millie, "Can you help me? This girl needs to have some fun in therapy."

I grabbed a small, soft kickball and placed it in Millie's lap as he sat in his wheelchair. "Hold this, please," I said.

Then I talked to the girl, whose mother had stayed for the session. "Could you help me? I need help throwing and catching the ball with Grandpa over there. I can't always aim that well." Then I went back to Millie, helped him stand up, and supported him as he and the little girl played catch.

For about twenty minutes, their laughs and giggles filled the department. When at last I sensed that Millie was tiring, I helped him back into his wheelchair. Then I heard the little girl run across the floor toward us. She hugged Millie, then me. It was beautiful, the full spectrum of children of God, both young and old, enjoying life.

On Millie's last day in the hospital, we worked together on a poem for our beautiful wives, so kind with special hearts and caring hands. I listened to his words, humbled once again by the way patients poured out their lives to me in their struggle to understand the split-second changes that come to us all. I gave him the only copy, but kept the memory of our working together to choose just the right words.

To those who wonder if their jobs give them the time to listen, I say that God gives us our time. If we can shorten the distance between God and someone else by listening to their stories, it's worth every minute.

*Good morning, dear Jesus. I ask and I pray
that you will be with us all through the day.
Help us to listen with all of our hearts,
in all that we do,
to be kind and responsible,
and more like you. Amen.*

22

When gazing at someone in a wheelchair or with a cane or someone who shuffles as she walks, it's easy to focus on the disability and miss the person. I often made this mistake with myself; caught up in dealing with my visual impairment, I forgot to focus on the person I was. A childhood memory and a conversation with Grandpa Meier changed my view.

Making Magic

I TRIED to make myself comfortable on the small classroom chair as Alea's first-grade teacher, Mrs. Cook, handed out sign-up lists. "Here are the various activities I need help with," she said.

"Could you tell me what's on it?" I asked. "I'm . . . visually impaired." Did she sigh or did I imagine it? She was a kind, loving, warm-hearted soul, but I was sure I could read her thoughts: *How could you possibly volunteer in my classroom, then? Of what earthly use could you be?* I wasn't sure how I would help, either. At first, I supposed I'd be like another student for her until she found ways for me to be useful.

I pointed out, "I can listen to beginning readers as well as anyone." With empathy, she agreed.

I must have passed muster during my first few visits to her classroom, because Mrs. Cook began letting me chaperone children who needed bathroom breaks and hand out papers for projects (I stood in one place and let the children come to me.)

Glad as I was to be of some help, I still felt rather invisible, more of a prop in her classroom than someone who really contributed. Then one rainy morning, when none of us could go outside for recess, I asked the little girl who was reading to me, "What's that behind your ear?" and pulled out a quarter. Then I flipped it through my fingers, a move my Grandpa Meier had made us all practice until it was as easy as blinking, and made it disappear.

The "Wow" that burst out of the little girl let me know I'd done it right. That set me thinking: How many of the other tricks Grandpa had taught us could I still use?

Grandpa Meier worked hard to put a bit of magic into every visit we made to his house. Sometimes Mom and all five of her children crowded into the living room for a real magic show.

"Feel inside the hat, Randy. Are you sure it's empty? Okay, I'll wave my wand over the hat and—alakazaam—Renay, what's in there?"

Even Mom laughed as I pulled out a stuffed bunny. Then Grandpa handed each of us a nickel. "Give them to Jocko. Put them right in his hand." Jocko, a toy monkey all dapper in top hat and red-and-white-striped vest, always served as Grandpa's "lovely assistant."

As hard as he tried, Jocko just couldn't grasp the nickels, so Grandpa tried to catch them as they fell to the floor. Then with a flourish he stretched out his empty hands, wriggled his shirt cuffs, and leaned over toward Jocko, as if listening to him. "Hmmm. Rhonda, Jocko thinks one nickel hid itself under that book on the TV."

Rhonda said, "It couldn't get way over there, Grandpa," but got up and checked. And, of course, there it was. Randy's nickel had almost made it out the front door and was hiding under the rug. Years went by before I figured out all of Grandpa's nickel tricks.

Other times he had little experiments ready to go. Mixing dyes to make new colors. Building "volcanoes" with baking soda. Flipping glasses without spilling water.

I'd always planned on using Grandpa Meier's magic with my own children. He'd taught us all the disappearing coin tricks and how to use his top hat, but I'd lost my sight before I had a chance to try anything with Alea or Kara.

I called Grandpa Meier the night the first grader had so enjoyed my coin trick. Grandpa said, "You know what else would be easy for you? Remember how to keep cotton balls dry in a glass of water?"

Grandpa's question let loose an explosion of ideas within my imagination. Why had it taken me so long to remember Grandpa Meier's magic? Mrs. Cook gave me permission to show the cotton ball trick to the whole class the next day. The children had such fun that the teacher suggested I come with a new idea each week.

The hands-down favorite of the boys was playing football. I hadn't lost my throwing accuracy from my high school quarterbacking days; I just needed to know where my target was. The boys stood around me in a circle. They took turns calling out and I'd pass it toward the voice. "I'm going out for a long bomb," they'd cry, and I'd heft the ball down the field. The boys never quite got over the magic of playing catch with a blind person.

I knew the teachers had grown comfortable with me when one day someone ran up to me in the midst of a recess game of catch. "All the teachers were having lunch," she said, laughing, "when someone looked out the window and said, 'Oh no, the blind guy's out there all alone with the kids!' It's hard to remember you really can't see!"

Grandpa Meier had a good chuckle at that one too.

Illusions and sleight of hand may seem childish to some, but for Grandpa Meier they were a way to be special to his fatherless grandchildren. For me, they were an avenue that helped children to see beyond my disabilities.

As I began my work at Sacred Heart, I used some of Grandpa Meier's tricks with my patients. When I went to the area where patients waited for their physical therapy appointments, I'd call a name. When the person answered me, I walked toward the voice. Often, the patients didn't realize I was blind until I asked them to help steer me down the hall. Their reaction? "Well, if you can do all this while you're blind, maybe I can get well, too!" I made it clear, though, that their courage and efforts usually far surpassed anything I had accomplished.

Once again, Grandpa Meier had reached out to help me, just as he'd cared for us, and every friend and neighbor he touched, all through our lives. When I was a boy I often wondered how he managed to show up to help mom just after the toilet backed up or the front door hinge cracked or a table leg took on a new wobble. Later, I understood that something always needed fixing and Grandpa delighted in taking care of it.

After I lost my sight, Grandpa had a couple of heart attacks. It was a heads-up for all of us that he wouldn't always be with us. He managed to stay in his little home for a while longer, aided by his daughter Bonnie who lived with him. The rest of us helped in any way we could. One afternoon, I followed his instructions to lift the motor off of his old fishing boat, a task he used to be able to do one-handed.

In 1993, Grandpa Meier's health deteriorated rapidly. Another heart attack placed him in a nursing home. I visited him as often as I could, listening to his misery: "I'm no use here. . . . I'm just a burden."

"The other residents don't think so," I said firmly. "All I have to do is mention your name and they laugh. They need your jokes; they'd like your magic tricks, too."

I shared all the ways his tricks were helping me. He chuckled when I described my quarterbacking adventures at the elementary school. "But I don't want to stay here," he said as I was leaving. "Can't you find a way to get me home?"

That was one piece of magic I couldn't seem to work. The twenty miles that separated our homes might as well have been a thousand, with me not being able to see. If I stayed with him, could I care for him? Yet Connie needed what help I could provide. His pleas tore at my heart. I said, "I don't see how, Grandpa. I wish. . . ." Not being able to help this man who had shepherded Mom and all of us rubbed salt in the wounds of my own battles with uselessness.

Late one night, Mom called to say, "Can you get to the Bloomer hospital right away?" Steve Trainor volunteered to drive me so that Connie could stay with the girls.

I joined my mother by Grandpa's bedside, rubbing her back while I held Grandpa's hand and told him, "I'm speaking for Randy, Rhonda, Shanon, and Kim. You poured out your life for us. We'll never forget all you did. It's okay, go home to heaven." A short while later, he went to be with the greatest Fisherman of all.

After Grandpa Meier's funeral, Randy, Uncle Gary, and I sat down out on the half wall of Grandpa's old house in

Bloomer. Lost in thought, I pulled up memories of the old garage where we'd hidden the ducks, the time Grandpa had let us paint his basement floor with sponges filled with green and yellow paint tied to our feet—Green Bay Packer colors. Suddenly, Randy exclaimed, "Oh, Renay—the northern lights are brighter than I've ever seen."

"I guess Grandpa's up there already," I quipped.

"Yep, doing magic tricks for the angels."

The feelings of being unable to help Grandpa come home lessened as I thought about where he was now, home for good. I didn't need to see the magic in the sky to say thanks to God for the magical light Grandpa Meier had added to my life, a light that helped me learn to believe in myself.

Children of God know the difference between maturity and mere atrophy of the imagination.

23

Unless you experience having a disability, all of the debate surrounding the labels may seem ridiculous. Blind? Visually impaired? Handicapped? The latter derives from "cap in hand," a phrase that was all too close to my feelings of uselessness in those first years of darkness. Firsthand, I learned the difference between being a visually impaired man and a person who is visually impaired. The latter recognizes that I am above all else a person, helping me focus on what I could do rather than what I could no longer do.

All new endeavors—and relationships—take time to succeed. We must be patient, yet persistent toward our goal. Instead of telling myself, "I'm blind," I chose to concentrate on the labels I'd given myself for years.

Old Roles, New Rules

"CAN'T NEVER DID NOTHING," I told myself. "Be a gardener or doom yourself to store-bought, plastic tomatoes."

As children, my siblings and I had fought over the juices left on the plate Mom used for slicing home-grown tomatoes, the winner flashing a smile of triumph before slurping with a sound that echoed throughout the house. I couldn't imagine a house without a garden, not after growing up with beans and lettuce and cucumbers fresh for the picking. Late summer afternoons and evenings found us canning beets, crushing berries for jam, and pouring brine into cucumber-stuffed jars while our mouths watered in anticipation of a winter full of pickles.

With dreams of digging potatoes once again, I mapped out a gardening plan. A neighbor loosened the soil for us with his rototiller. Connie purchased the seeds, twine, and extra stakes. And Alea became the best three-year-old helper anyone could ask for.

The biggest task was marking the rows so I wouldn't step on seedlings and so we could tell what was growing where. The yarn Connie found for marking the rows was thick and bright orange in color. I put stakes at each end of every row, then strung the twine between them. At planting time, the strings were close to the ground so that Alea and I knew just where to place the seeds. Then, as the plants grew taller, we moved the strings higher on the stakes.

That first year was a bit of a disaster; we got just enough tomatoes and beans, though, to make our efforts worthwhile. Further, I learned the value of an uncluttered garden.

The next year, I used a string that was knotted every two feet to lay out the rows. Alea did most of the planting, neatly placing the seeds at the intervals I demonstrated (I could tell how well she'd done when the plants sprouted). The first few weeks of cultivating were the hardest. I had a miniature rake that fit into the palm of my hand and I'd feel gingerly for the little seedlings while Alea helped to pull weeds and coached me, "Dad, your feet are getting close to the row behind us again."

I said, "Thanks, Alea. We can think of ourselves as seeds in God's garden. I wonder how we'll grow?"

"Big and strong, Daddy," she replied solemnly.

At harvest time, even Kara, now two years old, helped with the beans. I could hear the smiles in my daughters' voices as they ate their first bowls of beans that summer, sautéed with just a bit of butter and salt. In the years that followed, they often asked, "Can we go into the garden with our friends and get some green beans and carrots to eat?" I loved listening to them tell their friends about the role they played in gardening. Even though they didn't partake of everything we grew, they enjoyed repeating, "We've got Swiss chard, tomatoes, spinach, beets, parsnips, green peppers, cayenne peppers, peas, canning pickles, potatoes, carrots, beans, lettuce, and more, all in a sixteen-by-fourteen garden!"

MY NEXT QUESTION: Could I still be an electrician? I didn't want to say goodbye to the career I'd enjoyed so much. Jerry Woodford, my ride to Sacred Heart, felt the same way. He'd had to retire from electrical work due to rheumatoid arthritis and had actually helped me get an interview to take his place, the position that let me move to Eau Claire years before.

On our way to work one day, I said, "A few years ago, I could have wired a new outlet for our Christmas lights before breakfast. But now. . . ."

Jerry said, "I know what you mean. But you can't touch wiring without seeing it. I wonder. . . . My hands are as ill-suited to the work as your eyes. Maybe we're a match made in heaven."

"Do you think we could do it? Install that outlet on the front of my house, I mean?" I asked.

"As long as we're careful, the worst that could happen is having to call for reinforcements. What do we have to lose?"

The next Saturday, both of us got up on a ladder, with Jerry a couple of rungs below me. "Okay, reach to the left," he'd tell me. "That's your red wire. You've got it. Now, move your other hand up just a bit, now back. Okay, twist them together."

Believe me, no one else would have hired us—it took us days to do what we used to do in a couple of hours. But the thrill of victory was so complete that we forged ahead and installed backyard security lights as well.

I ALSO TOLD MYSELF, "I'm still a hunter." From the time Randy and I could aim a slingshot, our mom had depended on us to put meat on the family table. Money was that tight. Hunting wasn't a leisurely pastime for us but the difference between having bread and milk or having a real meal on many nights.

I met with a Department of Natural Resources ranger, Dave Rasmussen, who said, "Sure, you can hunt with a licensed partner." He took the time to pass on a few suggestions.

That question answered, I started my training. I tied a line with a pulley between the jungle gym and the tree. Then I attached a coffee can filled with rocks to a string. The girls operated the pulley, dragging the clanging can along the grass, while I aimed with my ears for it with a Nerf bow and arrow. It was elementary but effective. I needed to learn all over again, like a baby learns to walk.

Eventually, I trusted myself with the real thing, but not around Kara and Alea. Randy helped me figure out ways to shoot from a deer stand. The first trick was "spotting" a deer. In the woods where we'd hunted for years, my brother helped me run a piece of wire under the leaves along a deer trail to a "trip line" made of fishline. I attached the wire to a tiny 1.5 volt fan clipped to my jacket. In theory, when a deer tripped on the line, the fan would start. The line was far enough up the trail for me to have time to aim for a specific marked spot on the trail. Then Randy would help me aim for that mark, telling me to go left, right, or another direction. We never got a chance to try it out, though. While deer tripped the wire before hunting season, they all seemed to stay off the trail once November and the deer opener rolled around. Still, being out in the woods, reliving years of camaraderie with Randy, reinforced that there were still so many things I could do.

THEN CAME COACHING. When Alea started playing soccer, I volunteered as assistant coach, painting a ball fluorescent orange so that I could keep track of the action during practices. With my knowledge of strategies and positions, plus the enthusiasm that comes from cheering on your own children, I made myself quite useful. Occasionally, I had to laugh at myself, like the time I yelled, "Keep going, Alea, way to go," only to hear her say, "Dad, I'm not in right now. I'm standing beside you."

Being an athlete rose in importance when Connie, hesitancy in her voice, said, "Renay, you're losing that trim quarterback build with all of your good cooking. How about a tandem bike?"

I wasn't so sure. What if we got fifty miles from home and I strained a muscle or something? Would Connie be able to peddle both of us back home?

I kept my fears to myself, knowing that with that kind of caution we'd never have fun. We headed to a bike store. Connie told me, "There's a sturdy red one that I think we should try out." The store manager helped us wheel it outside and I found my way to the backseat.

The feel of peddling away, the wind in my face, without a care about where we were headed—I was hooked in an instant. Still, I wanted to check on whether Connie could handle peddling on her own. The road seemed to tilt upward; the pedals grew stiffer; we were headed up a steep hill. So, I lifted my feet off the pedals. I could hear my wife breathing hard, but she made it to the top.

Afterward I confessed and told her, "Connie, you really impressed me." I got a good shot to the ribs for making her work so hard.

GARDENER, hunter, coach . . . still, I couldn't do everything and anything, even if I set my mind to it with every ounce of strength in my heart and soul. I couldn't, in the whim of a moment, tell the girls to scramble into the backseat of our car for a hair-whipping drive through the fiery autumn countryside. I couldn't hop over to a neighbor's house to diagnose a wiring problem. I couldn't drive a boat while my girls learned to water ski. *Stop complaining about what you can't do and celebrate what you can! With your family and your faith, you're as lucky as any man alive.*

One winter day, the four of us piled into a car full of snow pants and extra mittens and headed for Christi Mountain, a local ski hill. Connie and the girls went with one instructor and another one was assigned to me. Years before, I'd skied the mountains of Colorado, but that day I spent hours on the bunny hill—how often we must crawl before daring to walk! Finally, my patient, caring instructor felt I was following directions well enough to venture onto a bigger hill. I kept asking, "Where are my girls?"

He said, "You don't need to worry—they're passing us, doing little jumps over piles of snow."

As I listened carefully for his shouts of "Right . . . left . . . right . . ." like a soldier marching for his country, I felt a sense of glory, and a closeness to Connie, Kara, and Alea.

Even though we weren't next to each other on the slopes, we were outside together in the world God created, and I was still very much a father.

God needs each of us to be the best we can be,
using our gifts as he intended,
not as the world suggests.

24

Once again, the events of what I thought would be an ordinary workday changed my life forever. . . .

Nothing Short of a Miracle

THE MORNING of May 23, 2000, Connie and I had breakfast together before I caught the bus for work. The radio announced, "Another picture-perfect spring day. If you're stuck in the office all morning, find an errand to run over the lunch hour that requires a walk."

Connie murmured, "Sounds like a good day to start planting the flowers. What should we put in the spot where the old maple tree used to be?" The fragrances of lilacs and lilies-of-the-valley made the flowers of spring still very much a treat for me.

I gave Connie a kiss, hugged Alea and Kara, then headed out, cane in hand, for the two-block walk to the bus stop. I could tell by the warmth on my face that the sun was out. At least three cardinals were calling back and forth to each other and I could easily picture their brilliant red feathers atop our neighbors' pine trees.

A cheery "Good Morning, Renay" greeted me at the bus stop. It was the ladies from the assisted living housing about a block from us. They always said hello, but one of them added, "It's gonna be a perfect day today."

She sounded so chipper that I replied, "It already is, don't you think?"

When the bus arrived and the driver opened the door, I thought I heard him whistling "Amazing Grace." It was that kind of spring morning, where the beauty of the weather and the fragrance of flowers and the chirping of the robins lets you know that life is good.

The bus dropped me off at Sacred Heart twenty minutes before my shift began. I took the elevator to the ninth-floor rehabilitation center. No one else was there yet, which meant I had a few extra minutes of solitude to get organized for the day. I made my way over to my station by the window and started cleaning the equipment with alcohol.

Suddenly, an intense pain filled my skull, as fiery as white-hot metal. I grabbed my head with both hands, then clutched at the windowsill to keep from tumbling to the ground. I panicked as I thought, *I must be having a stroke . . . and there's no one here to help me.*

Then a bright light flooded my eyes, the brightest light I'd seen since the accident ten years before. I continued to hold onto the window ledge, my heart pounding, my legs weak and trembling. Gradually, a soft, comforting feeling spread through my limbs, almost like a gentle embrace of love. The pain receded. Maybe I was all right?

As I straightened up, the bronzed cross that topped the hospital's chapel roof glistened in the sunlight. Dizzily, I thought that it looked like pure gold. Then it hit me: *I could see the cross!*

I was afraid to blink, afraid everything would go dark again. No, there were green leaves on the apple trees blowing gently in the breeze, a brilliant blue sky, puffy clouds streaming toward the sun—all of it more heavenly than any memory I'd cherished.

I stumbled backward, unable to think, and found myself leaning against the stairwell door. The stairs led right to the main floor chapel. Shouting, "I can see!" I raced down the nine flights of stairs to the first thing I'd spotted, that chapel, then fell to my knees in front of the altar, murmuring "Thank you! Thank you!"

The image of Bartemaeus on the street outside Jericho, so vividly described by that minister in Florida, flooded my brain. Bartimaeus shouting, "Lord, have mercy on me." I, too, had shouted for years and God had heard my prayers! Gratitude, joy, guilt at my joy, unworthiness, thanksgiving all jumbled together in my mind. Why me? Why this gift?

Slowly, I raised my head and looked around at the cross, the stained-glass windows I'd never seen before. Most of the blue-and-gold designs that rimmed the room's ceiling were abstractions, but here and there the distinct shape of an eye gazed down at me, all seeming to sparkle in the bright sunshine of that morning.

Perhaps I'd learned for good that dark, dark day on the riverbank that God had not deserted me, would not desert me, but seeing the brilliant eyes, seemingly the eyes of heaven, surround me, kept me on my knees in thankfulness for all the times God had held me through ten years of darkness. *Lord, you had mercy on me, a sinner!*

But then the bubble of joy inside me grew so intense that I had to tell someone—shout to the world what had happened. I walked—no, I floated—to the door of the hospital chaplain's office and pounded on it. I yelled much too loudly for a hospital corridor, "Father Klimek, are you there? I can see!"

"What? Come again?" I heard from behind the door. Then he opened it. Seeing that it was me, he put his hand on my shoulder and said, "What do you mean?"

I said, "I was wiping down the equipment upstairs when, all of a sudden, I could see the chapel cross. I can see."

He stared for a moment, then said, "Can you see the signs on the wall there?"

"Chapel, with an arrow to the right. Reception area, gift store, with an arrow the other way," I read as I pointed out directions. "Do you have a Bible I could read?" Then he threw his arms around me in a huge bear hug. Together, we walked back into the chapel, to the Bible on the altar. Together, we read aloud from Scripture, the first book I'd seen in ten years, John 14:27:

> *[Jesus said to his disciples:] "Peace I leave with you; my peace I give to you. Not as the world gives do I give it to you. Do not let your hearts be troubled or afraid."*

My voice broke. I stood and stared at the cross, then the stained glass, as Father Klimek continued to read.

When he stopped, I said, "Thank you, Father, for being with me. I'm sure you have things to do. I'll . . . I think I'll stay a moment more, if that's okay." I knelt to pray one more time.

But I couldn't stay still for long. I headed for the hallway. As I passed Father Klimek's office, I saw—I saw!—that some of the nuns were meeting with him. They stood up to greet me as Father Klimek reached for a phone and called the head of my department. "Renay's going to be a bit late this morning. Believe me, it's an excused absence!"

As he hung up, the sisters said, almost in unison, "Go outside and see what you've been missing." I didn't need to be told twice; I dashed out through the main hospital doors, stopping in front of the statue of Jesus, arms outstretched.

Surrounding the statue was a bed of red and purple and white flowers.

I dropped to the ground, too overwhelmed to take in all of the sights at once. Instead, I looked at a single flower, then another. A tiny bee caught my eye as it nestled into the petals of a brilliant daffodil. Then I flipped over and lay on my back, watching the clouds billow and pass by in the wind. I heard the sound of the flag whipping in the breeze and stared at the red, white, and blue, so familiar and yet so new to me. *Lord, to give me my sight on such a wondrous day—it's almost too much.*

Apple blossoms. A child holding onto her mother's hand. Cars—the cars looked different than the last time I saw a parking lot. Why, there was minivan after minivan. A moment of calmness spread through me as I pondered the wonder of everything in its place, every blade of grass, the trees gently moving with breeze, the blue sky—blue. I had forgotten what colors looked like!

I walked over to one of the apple trees, where ants crawled up the bark, perhaps moving toward heaven like my thoughts. That morning, everything stretching upward to heaven, just as my heart and soul and mind and body seemed to leap toward the sky. Everything was so beautiful, everything! I didn't see a thing that I didn't truly enjoy.

After a while I sat down on a bench outside the chapel, my mind overwhelmed with beauty. I didn't want to blink. I remember thinking, *Capture every detail. Maybe this is all temporary. You may be blind again when you wake up in the morning. Or, is this all a dream?* Those kinds of thoughts couldn't dampen my euphoria, though. When I looked at my talking watch, knowing the time without pressing a button, over two hours had passed! And I hadn't even called my wife!

I raced back to Father Klimek's office and phoned Connie, right in her classroom. I blurted out, "I can see again!"

"What do you mean?" she said quietly, as if her students were hard at work.

I told her what had happened. I wondered if the line had gone dead, it took her so long to answer. Then, a spark of hope in her voice, she said, "Should I come and get you?"

"Yes, no . . . I'd better get to work." *Or go home. Or call Mom. Or Gary. Or head to Alea and Kara's school. Or head out to Round Lake. Get on an airplane and fly around the world!* All these thoughts and more went through my mind in the span of about three seconds. I didn't know what I wanted to do. I told Connie, "Stay with your class for now, but meet me at home before you pick up our girls. I want to go with you."

I wanted to see my coworkers—Kay, Beth, and the others, so I headed up to the department, bounding up the stairs again to try to use up some of the energy that bubbled through me. By this time, most people around the hospital had heard that something had happened, but I could tell by their faces that they didn't understand just what. I gave out hugs and tried to match the voices I knew with the faces I'd never seen before. I couldn't focus on their questions; my mind was whirling, *This is where I work, but it's a brand-new world to me.*

"Go home, Renay," my boss said. "There must be something in the employee handbook about getting the day off if a miracle occurs." I nodded as best I could amidst the back-pounding and hand-shaking I was enduring.

Rather than make Connie call a substitute, I phoned my sister Rhonda. I think I repeated my story three times before she said, "Wait right there. I've got to see you for myself."

Within minutes, Rhonda and her husband Greg were at the hospital front door. They insisted on taking me out to lunch, asking where I wanted to go. "I don't care what I eat, I just want to read a menu for myself," I replied.

As I stared at the menu, Rhonda and Greg stared at me. "You can even read the fine print," my sister said in awe. "I don't believe this and I'm sitting right here, watching!"

Finally, I ordered a hamburger and a glass of milk. I said, "Tell me about my girls—describe them for me."

Rhonda tried, but I kept interrupting with questions. Finally, she asked "Don't you have pictures in your wallet or something?"

"Oh, yes!" I pulled them out, and stared. "It's unbelievable, how beautiful they are!" I perhaps heard mumblings from Rhonda and Greg, but I was lost in the moment. *These were my daughters.*

My hamburger and salad arrived. Green lettuce, a brilliant red tomato dotted with yellow mustard, a pickle with tiny white seeds nestled in the center. It looked so good that I hesitated before taking a bite.

Rhonda started telling a story about Mom, and I picked up my milk glass, swirling it slowly. The smooth whiteness of the whirlpool at the center of the glass amazed me. "Renay, are you all right?" Rhonda's voice broke through my thoughts.

"I'm more than all right—*everything* is magic. Think, ten years since I saw a bubble in a glass of milk, or could tell how much ketchup I'd scooped up with a fry."

They dropped me back at my home. I walked around the outside, seeing for the first time the jungle gym I'd built, its wood already weathering with age. The row of bushes in the backyard soared fifteen feet high; I used to keep them trimmed in a four-foot hedge. But this was home. The house, the lawn, the garden, my home sweet home.

I walked inside, to our kitchen. There was the glass-top stove, my good friend, but most beautiful of all was my daughters' schoolwork and artwork on our walls, the basement door, and the refrigerator. I peered at each paper, smiling at teacher comments such as, "Good work, Kara—A" or "Alea, this is very special."

Then I headed straight for the basement, for I knew exactly how I was going to spend the next few hours before Connie would be home. A huge chest held the family photo albums, copies of the girls' schoolwork, mementos of every memory our family had built together since the girls were born.

Pouring through the album pages, I saw Kara's baptism for the first time. Skating costumes, birthday parties, the First Communion dress both girls had worn, Kara kicking a soccer goal, Alea with her arms full of tomatoes from the garden, Connie and the girls in front of our Christmas tree. There was Kara in a little bunny suit, both girls sitting on the laps of Grandma and Grandpa Meier, a family party filled with nieces and nephews I didn't recognize. Again and again, I wiped my eyes to keep tears from falling on the pictures. I'd missed so many things. Or had I? I'd been there. I saw my own image throughout the books, but I glossed over them, intent on the photos of my girls. They were actually more special, more joyful than I had ever imagined.

In what seemed like just minutes, I heard a car in the driveway, the carpool Connie used to and from work. I was about to see my incredible wife. Was my face clean? My hair combed? I ran into the bathroom and looked at myself in the mirror for the first time in ten years: little hair, lots of wrinkles—"Aaagh, how I've changed!" My fingers had told me I was balding, but my goodness!

My own image made me wonder how had Connie changed. *Lord let my reaction be loving—no, I'll love my saint of a wife no matter what.*

The sight of Connie as she practically leaped from the car pool van left me speechless. Her twinkling eyes were just as I remembered, the smile that brightened her face and my heart—the only thing that had changed was her hairstyle!

"Oh, Renay," she cried as she took in how confidently I strode down our steps. We fell into each other's arms, but then I held her at arms' length for a long moment. She was so radiant that it took my breath away. If I hadn't been so anxious to see Alea and Kara, I'm not sure when I'd have let go. But we hurried to get the girls.

As they came out of our sitter's home, I stared and stared. They'd gotten so tall. They looked like beautiful flowers. I only stopped gazing at Alea's fine complexion and dance in her step to gaze at Kara's smile and self-assured gait, so like my sister Kim. Alea finally asked, "Dad, are you okay?"

"Alea, I'm looking at the most beautiful sight a dad can see."

"Dad, you're teasing us."

"No, I can see. I really can." As they scrambled into the backseat, I couldn't keep my eyes off of them. Alea stared back, her eyes sparkling, her mouth open just a crack in speechlessness.

Kara said, "Yeah, right, Dad." Then she took a piece of paper and some markers from her notebook, quickly sketched something, and handed it to me. "Dad, if you can see, then read this to me."

I smiled at the rainbow-colored hearts in each corner, then read aloud, "I love you Big Daddy. I love you Big Momma."

She stared at me for a second, then looked at her older sister and said, "Oh, oh, Alea, now we have to watch what we do around Dad!"

Connie and I laughed until the tears came.

WHAT DID WE DO that night? How could anything outside of us make the evening more special than it already was? We went to a doctor's appointment for Kara; she'd injured her finger. Home again, and everyone pitched in to make supper. I don't remember eating, just all of us looking at each other. I shot some hoops out in the driveway with the girls, enjoying the feel of my hands doing what my eyes told them to.

All of us knocked a volleyball, then a soccer ball, around in the backyard. We pulled lawn chairs up to the jungle gym platform and talked quietly about all the hours the girls had spent pretending it was a ship or a fort or a cabin. We stood by the garden fence and contemplated how we'd plant the best garden in the world, now that I could see.

Before bedtime, we looked at the pictures that I'd left scattered across the living room floor. Carefully, we each found a spot for sitting, then passed the best ones back and forth. There simply weren't enough for me to see!

As I tucked the girls into bed, I read several Bible verses and they joined in my nighttime prayer of thankfulness for what had happened.

Connie and I were exhausted as well. Seeing took so much energy, what with every sight new and refreshing. I was just a little afraid to close my eyes, wondering if I'd still be able to see in the morning. As I lay there, I remembered what I'd said to my girls ten years prior, on that day before Connie's birthday in 1990: "I'll see you tonight, Alea. I'll see you tonight, Kara." The day had passed. I can see them, they're beautiful. Thank you, God. Thank you for every single moment of my life.

If anything at all in life is true,
there is a miracle within you!

25

I'm still the boy from Bloomer, Wisconsin. I'm still a physical therapy assistant. I'm still husband to Connie and father to Alea and Kara. I'm still a child of God, learning what it means to trust God completely. In a flash of light, God drew me close, as if to say, "Go, tell others what you've learned about me. It's time. . . ."

. . . But Now I See

THE CRAZY THING IS, if you had interviewed me on May 22, 2000, when I still used a cane, when I still hadn't seen my family's faces in almost ten years, I'd have told you that I was happy. I'd put my trust in God, telling myself, *This is the way it's going to be from now on. Just do your best.*

I never stopped praying to regain my sight, but I'd found a full measure of contentment—my wife and children loved me, I saw my patients through my heart, I'd experienced firsthand the difference that faith makes in a world where God's love is our only certainty.

Yet now I had my sight as well. Those first days I could scarcely close my eyes, there was so much to see. I'd start to tell Connie about something, then I'd notice a picture or plant or book I hadn't seen before, and I'd break off in mid-sentence to investigate.

Each night, I fell into bed exhausted, overwhelmed, exhilarated, full of wonder, disbelief, and just a touch of fear over whether I'd still be able to see when I woke up the next morning. My ophthalmologist had told me, "Renay, you want to call it a gift from God. I would have to agree with you, because I can't figure it out either. Let's hope you keep seeing—I think you will."

My prayers were a jumbled mess. *Lord, thank you, I could never deserve such a gift. Please let me keep my sight. But, if things go dark again, help me bear it. And help me keep from dwelling on any fears—there's too much to see in your glorious world.*

The comments and opinions of friends, family, coworkers, and patients flowed freely. "Renay," so many said, "if anyone deserved such a miracle. . . ."

With total honesty, I replied, "I've done nothing that makes me more deserving of something this special than anyone else." I meant it. It took years for me to come to terms with my vision impairment. I was no saint; I wasn't worthy to wipe the sand from his sandals.

My mother could barely say anything other than, "Oh, Renay," when I told her that I could see again. When she found her voice, she told me, "I wonder. . . . When I made that very first trip to Europe last year, one of the reasons I went to Rome was to visit the Vatican. I wanted to pray for you at St. Peter's, and I did, gazing at the ceiling of the Sistine Chapel, in front of Michelangelo's *Pieta,* in the huge square where pilgrims gather on Easter and Christmas and other holy days."

Gary, who now lived in Wisconsin again, drove to Eau Claire as soon as he could. We danced around the living room, his joy every bit as overflowing as my own. The dance turned to prayer, then to laughter as we headed to Sammy's for a beef pizza. This time I could see how many meatballs covered my slices.

Eventually, the undertones of a different kind of reaction got back to me. *Renay wasn't any more devout or religious than other people.* To them I say, "You're right, I didn't deserve to see again. But God gives us great gifts whether we deserve them or not. We've all received Jesus, eternal life, the comfort of the Holy Spirit, no matter what we've done."

The only answer I've found to the question, "Why me," is that by May 2000, I'd discovered the truth that even in my darkness, God was still with me and my family. While I could never feel worthy of receiving a miracle, not with all of the needs and hopes of this world, I do know one thing— that no one would have listened to a blind Wisconsin electrician-turned-physical therapy assistant talk about how God helped him turn his life around. When I received my sight again, suddenly the whole world wanted to hear what I had to say.

Within a week of the accident, local reporters and photographers were at my door. The Eau Claire paper ran a front-page story about me on June 4. Then the *Today Show* called.

"We'd like to fly your family out right away to tape a show," they said.

Stammering in my shock that they had called, I replied. "Um, well, I'm sorry, that won't work this week," I replied. "Connie and the girls are visiting her sister in Colorado Springs. It's their special annual event." I couldn't think straight. Going to New York with my family would be so exciting, yet I couldn't interfere with Connie's trip.

The *Today Show* called back and their suggestion let me know just how far from home New York is for a boy raised in Bloomer, Wisconsin. "We'll send a Learjet to Colorado to pick up Connie and the girls, then to get you, and then on to New York."

I had to sit down; their excitement had my head spinning. "I can't say yes without talking to Connie, and she won't see her sister for another year." It still hadn't sunk in that the *Today Show* could possibly be interested in what happened to me.

The *Today Show* called a third time, and I finally grasped that people wanted to hear my story. The producer suggested, "Is there someone else you'd like to bring? We really want to feature you on our June 8 broadcast."

A few days later, Gary and Rhonda joined me on a trip to New York, along with a representative from Sacred Heart Hospital's communication department.

The day before the show was taped, we toured the Statue of Liberty, Ellis Island, Wall Street, Central Park, and Times Square. I still wonder how I looked to other people, craning my neck to see the sights, as excited as a six-year-old! On the observation deck at the World Trade Center, gazing out at New York and New Jersey and the ocean beyond, Gary said, "Imagine the view God has if we can see this much from here."

Near the World Trade Center, I spotted a beggar, leaning up against a cold, stone building, his arms folded over his knees, his hand outstretched, holding a tin cup.

I reached into my pocket, selected several bills, folded them into the man's cup, and said, "Can I sit down for a moment?"

He nodded, so I joined him in his house of cold concrete without even a chair to sit upon. I took in his walls of skyscrapers, the noises not of laughing children and a loving wife but of airplanes, and cars honking. He had no windows to open or to shut out the exhaust fumes.

Our time was short, but we talked of our families, our mothers and fathers. I told him, "I once was blind."

"You know, I once was as well," he answered. "I got caught up in the rat race of life in this town."

I had time to hear a little more of his story, but when I started to shake his hand to say good-bye, he reached into his cup and forced my money back into my hand. "Thank you for talking to me. Nobody does that anymore. That is far more a treasure to me than money."

Gently, I placed the bills back in his cup and said, "And for me as well. May you somehow be blessed as God has blessed me." We parted with a gentle hug. As I glanced back over my shoulder, at a distance, I saw a ray of sunlight streaming down the side of the building toward him and he smiled.

I walked away, again overwhelmed at the enormity of the gift God had given me. Why had I received my sight? I was probably less deserving of a miracle than the man I'd just met.

Yet because I regained my sight, I've gotten to tell my story on *Oprah*, in *People Magazine*, *Guideposts*, on *20/20*, *It's a Miracle, Dr. Schuller's Hour of Power* broadcast from the Crystal Cathedral—over 150 media opportunities broadcast in 175 countries, traveling from New York to California, from Texas to Minnesota. Everywhere, I met wonderful, kind, caring people who are seeking to show God's love to the world. I'm invited to tell about the events of May 23, 2000, but I also get to tell about how I learned to see through the eyes of God, how I found a new life even in the darkness, while I was still blind.

A crew from *20/20* spent three or four days in Eau Claire, listening to my story, filming Connie and the girls, sights at Sacred Heart and other places. I had asked them to be extremely considerate of Alea and Kara, because Kara had been startled by a cameraman just a few days before; our family was getting a bit overwhelmed by all of the media attention.

The whole crew was wonderful. The reporter, Bob Brown, spent hours helping Kara perfect her curve ball and demonstrating soccer tips to both girls. Trish Arico bent over backward to allow our family to tell of our struggles with my vision loss, and the gift we received, my sight.

After several months of intense media attention, we tried to return to some semblance of normalcy by keeping Connie and the girls out of the spotlight. There were so many other things we longed to do together: bike across the countryside, go fishing and have all four poles in the water, head back to Country Fest where I'd now be able to see the stage—*Lord, do people know how much splendor there truly is to see in your world? Thank you, thank you. Amen.*

Will I sleep or will I wake?
If I wake, will I see and hear?
If I see, will my heart be big enough to
act for the good of all?
For this I pray. Amen.

Passing on the Gift

THE GIFT STORE at Sacred Heart stocks a jar with handmade caramels that rival those from the old Grenache's Candy Store in Superior—that crystal coating on the outside and creamy, soft inside. I often get the urge to buy a dozen or so. I untwist the waxed paper from one and take a bite, letting the sweet morsel melt in my mouth. Then I tuck four in my pocket for my family and me to enjoy that evening. They're just as much a favorite for Connie, Alea, and Kara as they are for me.

But I still have seven left, so my search begins for people whose lives need a touch of sweetness. I may not get any farther than the hospital lobby before I spot someone I know.

Sometimes it's a former patient whose spouse now has cancer.

Or a woman from my church who's visiting her mother in intensive care.

On a joyful day, it's a neighbor wheeling his wife and newborn child out to greet the world as a family.

Or, with a somber prayer, I might tuck one into the hand of a friend who just received bad news.

It's such a simple thing, but an amazingly effective way for me to show that I care, that God cares. The ordinary waxed paper lets people know that inside is something special; not just any candy would produce the smiles and laughter that my caramels do.

My little caramel ritual reminds me over and over that in all days and in all ways, I need to pass on the great gift that God gave me—not just my sight, but the knowledge planted deep inside of me that God is always with us, waiting to show us the light of heaven, of love, of life, even in our darkest moments. May that light always shine for you.